RETIREMENT
TRAVEL

by
Lauren West

Wasteland Press
www.wastelandpress.net
Shelbyville, KY USA

Retirement Travel:
Cheap, Easy, Fun!
by Lauren West

Copyright © 2020 Lauren West
ALL RIGHTS RESERVED

First Printing – July 2020
ISBN: 978-1-68111-358-6

NO PART OF THIS BOOK MAY BE REPRODUCED IN ANY FORM, BY PHOTOCOPYING OR BY ANY ELECTRONIC OR MECHANICAL MEANS, INCLUDING INFORMATION STORAGE OR RETRIEVAL SYSTEMS, WITHOUT PERMISSION IN WRITING FROM THE COPYRIGHT OWNER/AUTHOR

Printed in the U.S.A.

0   1   2   3   4   5

I'm dedicating this book to my son, Matt Crockett - he has been trying to get me to write a book for ages - and my younger sister, Terry Lynne Sanders, because it wasn't her initial idea to write a book, but she "sold" me on it. They are my biggest fans. I love you both!

ACKNOWLEDGEMENTS

My appreciation first goes to Buck Custer for reading my first chapter and encouraging me to continue. Buck read my first and last draft and is still encouraging me and helping me edit it all.

Thanks to my sister, Terry Lynne and son Matt for having faith in me that I could do this and picking up the editing job from where Buck left off.

Thanks to Joe and Matt for providing transportation to and from the airport for my trips. I know it wasn't always convenient but they took the time to do it anyway. I Love you guys.

TABLE OF CONTENTS

CHAPTER ONE: *Love of Travel* 1

CHAPTER TWO: *Too Broke to Pay Attention!* 4

CHAPTER THREE: *Bribes Anyone?* 9

CHAPTER FOUR: *Magnets, T-shirts and Mugs* 12

CHAPTER FIVE: *AFVC – What's That?* 14

CHAPTER SIX: *The Twelve Days of Christmas* 16

CHAPTER SEVEN: *More to Las Vegas than the Strip* 21

CHAPTER EIGHT: *17 Days, 4 Countries with Only a Carry-On* 24

CHAPTER NINE: *Real Women Don't Pay Full Price!* 28

CHAPTER TEN: *My Dream Cruise – I Can't Miss My Ship!* 31

CHAPTER ELEVEN: *That's Your Uniform?* 43

CHAPTER TWELVE: *Who Says People in New York/New Jersey Aren't Friendly?* 48

CHAPTER FOURTEEN: *Toronto – Niagara Falls* 55

CHAPTER FIFTEEN: *Las Vegas – Red Rock Canyon – Online Dating* 65

CHAPTER SIXTEEN: *Handy Hints and Packing, I'm No Expert!* 69

CHAPTER SEVENTEEN: *Las Vegas – Grand Canyon* 73

CHAPTER EIGHTEEN: *Freeport Isn't Across the Bridge from Nassau?* 78

CHAPTER NINETEEN: *Myrtle Beach – Let's Shag!* 83

CHAPTER TWENTY: *10 Day Southern Caribbean Cruise on RCCL* 90

CHAPTER TWENTY-ONE: *Breaking Out of Rehab* 98

CHAPTER TWENTY-TWO: *Free Week in Mazatlan* 104

CHAPTER TWENTY-THREE: *Reno, Nevada – Built In Tour Guide* 110

CHAPTER TWENTY-FOUR: *The End of My Retirement Trips... NOT!* 115

MY CRUISE HISTORY 120

CITIES I'VE VISITED IN 2½ YEARS 122

CRUISES IN RETIREMENT THE LAST 2½ YEARS 125

CHAPTER ONE
Love of Travel

My love of travel started when I was a small child. I came from a middle class family, or I thought I did. There were four kids in our family and my Father (I called him Dad or Daddy) supported us on his income alone. My Mom was a nurse but quit nursing when she married my Dad (old habits are hard to break, I'm still calling him Dad). They had what I called the "old school" type of marriage. Dad worked, brought home the paycheck, and Mom did everything else, including helping Dad with his job or business.

I didn't see it or think it at the time, but they must have really loved us kids and each other. They always made sure we got everything we needed and wanted. You might have to wait till payday, but we got it. Dad was paid weekly. Every Friday. I think he was making $100 a week at that time. 1957 - 1962.

My Dad served in the Army during World War II. He was a Sergeant and a radio operator. Dad loved to travel, so I think I got that honestly. I was born in Shreveport, Louisiana. We moved to Twin Falls, Idaho when I was three. From there we moved to San Diego, California when I was four or five. We moved back to the South and I started first grade in Marshall, Texas. We then moved back to San Diego when I was in third grade and stayed there, although not in the same house or part of town, till the middle of my 9th grade, when we moved back to Shreveport. I kicked and screamed and started my years of rebellion with that move. Talk about a culture shock. From San Diego to Shreveport. I graduated high school from Woodlawn High School in Shreveport in 1966. I was afraid they were going to give me a blank diploma at graduation. I didn't care about grades, I just wanted out of school.

Wherever we lived, we took an annual vacation. It was always a car trip. If we lived in California we would go south, usually to see family. If we lived in the South, we would go west and see family. Dad always made our trips fun. We would get to sleep in a motel if we didn't drive straight through. We got to eat out and stopped to see sights to and from. Occasionally, we would have picnics in the car or at a park on the way. Dad would stop at a store, go in and buy a loaf of bread, bologna, a jar of mayonnaise, and a carton of milk. Those bologna sandwiches were the best ever. Knowing Dad, he probably bought a bag of cookies too. He always had a sweet tooth and he also knew us kids would be thrilled.

I remember one stop was in Tombstone, Arizona. We got to go in a real saloon, went to the old cemetery and read what was on the headstones and "did the town". I was nine years old, but I will never forget it. Westerns were very popular in those days and we watched them all on one of our three channels we got on TV. I will always remember one tombstone. It had the name of the deceased and under the name it said, "Hanged by Mistake". There were many funny epitaphs.

Three of us kids were in the back seat. My older brother Jimmy, who always sat by the window behind the driver, my older sister Linda, who sat by the window on the passenger side and me, the baby for nine years before "the Brat" was born. I sat in the middle of the back seat, leaning on the front seat. My baby sister Terry Lynne was in the front seat with Mom and Dad. There were no seat belts in those days. Someone was always bothering the other person. Sitting too close, rolling the window all the way down with the wind blowing on the others, touching one another, etc.

When we were traveling we played games like "Twenty Questions" and sang songs. We were a musical family and we would harmonize. To break the monotony, my sister and I would occasionally hit a note just a little flat, "just to get my Dad's goat". He would say, "now damn it, if you aren't going to sing right, then don't sing at all." We were laughing and punching each other in the back seat. A couple of our favorites were, "I've been working on the Railroad" and "You are my Sunshine". Sometimes out of boredom we would sing extremely fast. Try singing "The Battle of New Orleans" in double or triple time.

When at home, various instruments were played. Dad played guitar, harmonica, and banjo. He could play the guitar, sing, play the banjo, play the harmonica with his nose, and tap his foot at the same time. He was always the life of the party when Mom and Dad had company over on most Saturday nights.

My Dad worked in electronics. At more than one time, he had a television repair shop, but could do any electronics repairs, and he made a living doing this.

He opened a CB radio shop in Shreveport in 1963 and built, sold, and repaired CB and Ham radios. Dad didn't even finish high school, but did all this and more. When we lived in San Diego, he repaired jukeboxes and pinball machines. He worked on police radios, CB radios, and built devices for private detectives for surveillance. We didn't recognize it at the time, but I think he was the closest thing to a genius you could ever meet. If it was electronic, he could figure it out.

CHAPTER TWO

Too Broke to Pay Attention!

Before I start telling you of my retirement adventures, I want to tell you how I got to the place in my life where I could do this.

I'm a single female, 71 years old and raised two sons pretty much on my own. My sons were each raised as an only child; there are twenty years difference in their ages.

When I was 43, I was divorced and living in Los Angeles. I worked for Stone Container Corporation as a customer service rep in the Multiwall Bag Manufacturing plant.

When I first moved to Los Angeles, I was living in a hotel and would tell people I was "a homeless bag lady". I married Matt's father and, although I had a good job, I didn't feel I was doing anything that had a meaningful purpose in my life. I prayed God would give me a purpose.

Well, be careful what you pray for! At 43 years old I got pregnant. I was not only in shock, I was in denial. I had just gotten my older son, Joe, raised and in college, and then bam! I had to start all over again!

There was never a question in my mind that I was going to have this baby. The scary part was that I was 43 and worried he might not be perfect! Whatever the future held, I would face it. I believed with all my heart that if God was going to give me a baby, at that age, he would provide for it.

When Matt was born, I asked "Is he okay?"; I was afraid to look at Matt till his father told me he was perfect. I had a new purpose in my life!

Matt was a gorgeous baby and a beautiful child. I doted on him and so did his father. Matt's father and I divorced when Matt was a year old.

I moved back to Arkansas to be closer to my older son and so Matt and Joe would know each other.

Matt's father, "Davy Crockett", only paid child support for nine months. He always knew I would see to Matt's needs and wants. When Matt was two years old, David started watching him while I worked. That made up for the child support.

His Dad was in college and would take Matt with him to his classes. I always said Matt had more college hours than anybody I knew without getting a degree.

Matt started kindergarten at 4 years old and I only had to pay for before and after school care. Here I was paying four student loans for my older son's college tuition and room and board and paying before and after school care for Matt. I always said "I was so broke, I couldn't pay attention."

If you are thinking this book is written by a well kept wife, lunching at the club and her main purpose in life was to get her nails done, think again. (Although, I do get my nails done. My one extravagance.)

I never applied for or accepted any kind of assistance. I worked. I always had a full time job and most of the time two part time jobs in addition. I did demos at grocery stores, or sold cappuccino at local venues for broadway plays when Matt was at his Dad's for visitation every other weekend. Matt would go with me when I distributed posters for Celebrity Attractions in exchange for show tickets and I did fragrance demos at Dillards on his Dad's weekends. I cleaned my friends house for thirteen years which was a real lifesaver. Matt went with me. That job helped pay for daycare.

I said all this not to pat myself on the back, but so you would understand you don't have to be rich or win the lottery to travel. Friends, church members and acquaintances are always asking me if I won the lottery! Not hardly. Like everyone else who buys a lottery ticket, I have a plan if that happens, but travel wasn't at the top of the list. You can also count on less than two hands how many lottery tickets I've purchased. One can always dream.

Let's get down to the "nitty gritty". I went to work as a contractor to the National Guard. I was hired as an office manager. There wasn't much to manage, so I looked for other things to not only keep me busy but give me a little job security.

I developed the "Help Desk Coordinator Position". I answered calls coming in the office from students that attended classes but needed functional and technical assistance with the systems after they returned to their home states. I logged the calls and assigned them to the appropriate Instructors/Analysts.

I'll never forget learning to use the fax machine. The guys told me to dial 9, pause, and then dial the area code and the phone number. So I hit the 9 button and "paused" (or hesitated, throwing my arm out like Vanna White on Wheel of Fortune as if to say "ta da", but without saying "ta da"). I then proceeded to dial the number. It still didn't work, so the guys said, "What are you doing?" I showed them by repeating the process, exaggerating the "pause". They all fell out laughing! They explained that there was a "pause" button. Talk about a blonde moment. Did I tell you I was a blonde?

After nine months, I was encouraged to apply for an Instructor position. Me teach Logistics? I didn't know what SPBS-R, ULLS-S4 or SARSS even meant, much less know the military acronyms. They might as well have been speaking Greek. The other Instructors said, "We'll train you!"

So the number one person I have to thank for giving me the opportunity that changed my life is Gary Miner. Mr. Miner was my boss and he gave me a shot at teaching. I didn't start out making instructor pay but I was at least headed in that direction.

I worked on a team with two other Instructors that taught me the two systems I was going to be teaching for the next several years. Dave Davidson and Robert Spencer were "my" Instructors.

We had a great time in class and I learned so much from both of them.

I had challenges as a single parent that others didn't have. I was taking a Distance Learning Class and the instructor told us we could stay till 10 p.m. to do our project and use the classrooms equipment. I asked what we should do if we had to be at our daycare by 6 to pick up our children? He responded, "Suck it up cupcake." So, I picked up my five year old son at daycare and used my own video camera to tape record my five year old demonstrating using the VCR, microwave oven, television, etc. and built my presentation around the current technology. I "sucked it up".

I no longer dreaded the school year starting. I could afford school supplies and uniforms for Matt. I could afford health insurance finally! So thank you Mr. Miner!

I didn't get rich, but my life was less stressful. Like I said earlier, I always knew if God was going to give me a baby at that time of my life, he would provide for us. Thank you God.

A couple of years before I started work as a contractor, I bought a house. Not a big house, but big enough for me and my two sons.

My co-worker, Mike Maynard, one of the smartest men I've ever known, would teach me things in the downtime between classes. He talked to me about paying off my house in 15 years instead of 30 years. He gave me precise instructions on how to accomplish this. Starting off with how I should make at least one extra payment a year, make additional payments to go to principle each month and refinance if I could find a lower percentage rate. I refinanced twice and paid off my house in 15 years instead of 30 years. Thank you Mike Maynard.

Last, but certainly not least, my co-worker Paul McDaniel and I had many conversations and one particular conversation was about his and his wife Sharon's plan for their retirement. He said their goal was to be "Debt Free". I'd never even thought of anything like that. He explained how they planned to accomplish that and I decided I wanted to do the same thing. That sounded pretty cool. If I was debt free I wouldn't have to work forever and I could someday retire on my savings and social security.

I paid off my house three years before I retired and put the payments I would have been making into my savings. I collected Social Security two years before I retired and I also put all that into my savings. My cars were paid off and I have no credit card debt. My only bills are utilities, real estate taxes and insurance. If you can show me a way to avoid those bills… I will gladly listen!

I have one credit card and I only use it when I have the money to pay for those items. I pay my credit card off within three days of charging on it. I only use it for the points. I pay "no interest" and keep a zero balance.

I have a Carnival MasterCard and have taken 30 Carnival cruises since 1980. I get money back for my points and use it for on board credit on my cruises.

Thank you Paul McDaniel for telling me about your "debt free" plan.

CHAPTER THREE
Bribes Anyone?

AFVC - Armed Forces Vacation Club. I will talk about it later at length, but this is how I book my condos when I travel. Fully furnished condos for $349 for a 7 day stay.

Yes, I said bribes. In Mexico they actually referred to the gifts, breakfast/lunch given you in exchange for a tour of a property along with a "sales pitch" to buy a condo as "bribes".

The resorts make their money by selling weeks in their condos and are willing to compensate you for your time. You might be offered cash, credit at your resort to pay for food, drinks, show tickets, bottles of tequila, tours of the city, dinners, and even a free week stay at another resort in another city. If you are willing to devote a couple of hours, you can get some pretty nice gifts. You don't have to buy to get the gifts, but there are some pretty good sales people that convince hundreds of people to buy.

I don't usually mind giving up a couple of hours in exchange for cash or some very nice gifts. I was staying at a gorgeous resort in Cabo San Lucas and was given a $350 credit at my resort for taking a tour to a sister resort and having a wonderful buffet breakfast and listening to their sales pitch. At the end of my week, my bill was $47. That was for gratuities. They didn't allow gratuities to be paid with your credit. I had a breakfast every day at the resort, eggs benedict, drinks and lunch by the pool. dinners and even steak and lobster the last night of my stay. What a deal.

One time in Puerto Vallarta I was given 2000 pesos, 2 bottles of tequila, a massage, transportation to and from my massage and transportation to and from the airport. I was in Puerto Vallarta from Saturday till Thursday before I spent a penny of my own money. 2000 pesos was the equivalent of $200 U.S.

When you tour the resorts, the condos are their top of the line condos and are decorated beautifully and are true luxury accommodations. Some have not only a private hot tub, but private pool as well.

Over the last two years I've been given resort credits, show tickets, cash, liquor, tours, gift cards, week stays at other resorts and usually a lovely breakfast or lunch. Not bad for investing two hours of my time.

The sales reps are usually very nice and the properties are lovely. Why would I pay $50,000 for a condo, and on top of that, pay an annual maintenance fee when I don't have to.

My condo in Cabo San Lucas was exceptionally nice. Not only did I have a junior suite with partial kitchen, two queen size beds, living area with sofa, loveseat and two coordinating chairs and coffee table and end table, but a balcony that was 12 x 20 with padded lounge chairs, and table and chairs.

I was laying out by the pool one day and was looking at all the balconies. With the exception of about four balconies, the other balconies had room for a small table and two chairs, and that was it. Wow. How did I luck out and get that huge balcony? My balcony was facing the pool and had a beautiful ocean view. It looked like something you would see on a postcard.

My maid would do all kinds of cool things with making the towels, kleenex, and toilet tissue look like flowers. Just small thoughtful touches to make you enjoy your condo and feel special.

When I walked in my condo, one of the beds had a design on top of it that was made of turquoise glass beads that followed the color scheme of the condo and said "Welcome" with a pretty design under it. What a nice thing to have as a welcome. I didn't want to disturb it and always slept in the other bed.

I am kind of a neat freak, so making up my room daily is not hard for the maids. I make up my bed, pick up after myself and leave my room as I found it when leaving to tour or lay by the pool for the day.

The maid brings in fresh towels, and remakes the bed, and adds special touches each day, like a towel animal, or a flower on top of the kleenex holder made of kleenex, the washcloths folded into a fan, etc. It doesn't take much to make me happy. I love and appreciate all those special touches and usually leave a Thank You note with a tip at the end of my stay.

CHAPTER FOUR

Magnets, T-shirts and Mugs

What's the fun of traveling if you can't bring home souvenirs and keepsakes as a reminder of the great trip you had?

With the exception of one trip, I always brought home souvenirs. Usually, this consisted of T-shirts for my sons, daughter-in-law, grandson, former co-workers, friends, and my precious "nail tech", Hong.

My friend and former co-worker, Tammy Farrar, collects magnets, so I have made it a point to bring her a magnet from all the cities or countries I visited since retirement 2 1/2 years ago. She has an entire door devoted to the magnets I brought her. I call it my "retirement door". Anytime I cruised, I would bring her a magnet from the ship as well. Magnets are a pretty inexpensive souvenir. They range from $2.00 to $6.00 usually.

My son Matt, collects coffee mugs. When Tammy gets a magnet, Matt gets a mug, even if nobody else gets a souvenir. He has quite a collection. I wish he had them displayed so I could get a picture. I think the prettiest and most unusual, as well as the most expensive cup, was from "The Eiffel Tower" in Paris. I purchased it on a 17 day trip to four countries using only a carry-on. I didn't have room for souvenirs, but brought back magnets and that one mug. That was so hard to do. I went to Paris, London, Dublin, and Glasgow and couldn't buy souvenirs!

My friend Tim collects T-shirts, so I bring him a nice T-shirt almost everywhere I go. He says he won't have to buy a T-shirt for the rest of his life because of all the T-shirts I've bought him.

I did buy myself a T-Shirt in Dublin and had to wear it home because there was no room for it in my carry-on.

CHAPTER FIVE
AFVC – What's That?

Check out AFVC.com, look at Space A, Click on destinations and see all the available resorts listed by country, state and availability.

Unless I was on a cruise, I usually booked trips a week at a time through Armed Forces Vacation Club. They have resorts all over the world. You can pay a lot to stay at these resorts, or you can do it like I did. I searched for resorts in what they call $349 Space-A. These are properties that are not already booked by the owners of the condos in these resorts. They have hotel rooms and one, two, and sometimes three bedroom condos.

I can stay at a beautiful resort for seven days for $349. There are no other fees, no maintenance fees and I just pay when I want to go. I've booked everything from a hotel room to a two bedroom-two bath condo with full kitchen and, most times, even a washer and dryer.

Some resorts, especially in Mexico, have daily maid service and some even offer turn down service in the evening like they do on a cruise ship. Typically in the States, daily maid service is available at an additional charge.

The kitchens are fully equipped. You could bake cookies if you want. All dishes, pots and pans, coffee maker and microwave ovens are furnished as well as an ample supply of towels. I don't usually cook, but I love having the refrigerator and microwave for drinks and snacks or any take-out brought back to the condo.

Most resorts offer shuttle service to shopping areas and places of interest to visit. Sometimes there is a minimal charge if say, you wanted to take the shuttle to Red Rock Canyon just outside of Las Vegas. If you want to be dropped off at the strip or a shopping center the trip is free and there is a schedule available when you check in.

Resorts have pools, on site gyms, and sometimes parties and activities for the residents. I've been to barbeques by the pool, breakfast, and parties at their restaurants and bars.

My trips to Puerto Vallarta, Cabo San Lucas and Mazatlan, Cancun, Cozumel, and Playa Del Carmen are at beautiful resorts and are booked through AFVC.

AFVC offers 200,000 resort accommodations in over 100 countries. High Demand inventory represents a broader range of resort availability, including peak travel times, larger units and more sought after destinations.

Check out AFVC.com. Short stay inventory is available for less than a week. They also have mandatory and optional All Inclusive resorts as well.

Booking the $349 stays afforded me the opportunity to take a trip a month for the last 2 1/2 years. Before I retired, I had the first six months booked. I got some amazing deals.

AFVC membership is available to military, retired military, and employees of DOD and their families. Gift certificates can also be purchased and given to non-members.

CHAPTER SIX
The Twelve Days of Christmas

My son Matt had friends in Mexico that he met in college and they wanted to do a trip together and do 12 cities in 12 days in Mexico in December 2016. They asked me to join them. That was right up my alley, so the planning started. There would be four of us and we would start in Cancun and work our way South. I made reservations for all 12 nights, some prepaid. Then Matt's friends decided not to go!

We already had non-refundable airline tickets to Cancun and I wasn't about to lose over $800, so I made changes and booked hotels in Cancun for 3 Days, Cozumel for 6 days and the last 3 days in Playa del Carmen for just Matt and myself.

We left Little Rock on December 16th and flew to Cancun and found our hotel. We were going to be gone for 12 days, so five star hotels were not on our agenda. The hotels were nice enough, although not even a chain hotel like Holiday Inn or Hampton Inn. They were really kind of cute.

The first hotel had a restaurant and a pool, AC, and was very clean, if not fancy. It had security, so that was a plus.

On the third night we went to the tourist area of Cancun. We took a bus that was about a 30-minute ride.

We first went to an open-air nightclub that had a ticket that gave you "all you can drink" and then you could go across the street to Coco Bongo. You didn't get all inclusive drinks at Coco Bongo, so you made the most of it at the first nightclub. Maybe I should clarify that, Matt made the most of "all you can drink". I had a couple of drinks.

The first club was packed and had three stations designed for what we used to call "go-go dancers".

The dancers wore one piece black and white bodysuits, showing lots of hips and legs and wearing thigh-high black boots. Needless to say, they could really dance and were very attractive. The streets were jammed and you could see all the activity in the bar to include those go-go dancers from the street. The dancers were right by the sidewalk!

Our tickets for Coco Bongo were for entrance from approximately 10 to 11 p.m. We walked in and were escorted to the show area. It was three stories, with a stage, a huge screen behind it, a bar in the center of the floor and wall to wall people. There had to be a couple of thousand people in that club. The music was "rockin", and everyone was singing along and dancing. It was amazing! We wanted to sing along but it was all in Spanish. There were three floors and we were on the bottom floor. At times there was entertainment on the stage, film behind it, and a show with acrobats flying overhead, landing in the middle of the club, doing acts that look like superheroes fighting. Maybe every 30 minutes, alarms would start blaring, confetti and streamers dropped from the ceiling. It was wild!

We met some young ladies and their friends. Matt is like me, he rarely meets a stranger. Matt and I danced both swing and freestyle. We had a lot of fun dancing, even in those crowded conditions. He even dipped me.

Matt's a good looking guy, 5"10, gorgeous head of dark hair and beautiful green eyes. All through school he was kidded about his long eyelashes. He hated it. He is not only good looking but he's a sweet guy. He has tons of friends that are girls as well as guy friends.

He always meets young ladies wherever we go. He's a good dancer and they love to dance with him. He loves to "twirl" them if its a swing or a salsa and they love it.

Matt speaks Spanish, maybe not fluently, but he can communicate pretty well.

I was pretty tired by 3:30 A.M. so I decided to go back to the hotel. Matt stayed. Of course. I tried to find a bus, but gave up and took a taxi. I thought maybe it would be safer than wandering the streets in Mexico alone at 3:30 in the morning. I made it back to the hotel just fine.

Matt called at 5 A.M. and said he was going with the young ladies he met, to a house party. Oh my God! Going to someone's house he just met, to a party in Mexico! That would not be unusual in Little Rock. But we were in Mexico!

I finally said okay, but told him we had a shuttle at 8:30 A.M. to go to the ferry to get to Cozumel and he better be back to the hotel in time. I started praying that he would make it back safely to the hotel, then I tried to sleep. Right.

Let me regress... Before we left on our Mexico trip my older son, Joe, told us we better be careful. He didn't want to get a ransom call because we were kidnapped! We laughed about that. Joe is a lieutenant at the sheriff's department and is always thinking about safety or crime.

I shrugged that off because I've been to Mexico many times alone and never had a problem. I always say "You can get killed in Little Rock."

Matt showed up at 7 a.m. I told Matt I was going downstairs and order breakfast and for him to get showered and dressed. I laid out his clean clothes. I told him to pack his things and come downstairs. He was still a little inebriated. That's probably an understatement.

I ordered breakfast and went to the lobby and waited for Matt. I called the room and I told Matt to get his butt down to the lobby! He apparently fell asleep so he was confused, I guess.

All of a sudden he knocked on the lobby door. It was locked, I guess for security reasons. I looked at Matt. He is standing there barefooted, no shirt, and wearing only boxer briefs.

I looked at him, shocked, and said "Where the hell are your clothes?!" Matt said, "I got a ransom call to come to the lobby." I said, "That was me, dumbass."

I asked him where his clothes were. He pointed to an open hallway about 15 feet from the door. There sat his luggage.

I told him to get his butt over there and get dressed! This was all done in like a stage whisper because there were other people in the lobby.

I left my luggage in the lobby and ran back up to the room to see if he left anything. Of course he had. I got his shaving gear, his electric toothbrush and other toiletries he had left in the bathroom.

So the shuttle arrives and we were the only passengers. I was laughing hysterically over what just occurred. Matt was leaning over, trying to sleep and he kept saying ugly things to me, that I won't repeat here. I was telling him to stop because it wasn't very nice. So he started flipping me off. That made me laugh even harder. Oh my God. You've got to love sons.

We made it to the ferry and Matt behaved while waiting in line. When we were boarded, there was a huge section with five seats across. Matt took up most of one row by laying down and sleeping for the approximately 45 minute ride to Cozumel. Of course I'm taking pictures of him all sprawled out sleeping. I'll never let him live it down. Ever. Too funny.

I've always bought gifts for the 12 Days of Christmas because, when Matt was little, he would start in, several days before Christmas wanting to open a gift. So I bought gifts for the Twelve Days of Christmas, so he would have a gift to open each day. These were like stocking stuffers, nothing big.

Since we would be traveling, I decided to give him a handwritten card every day instead of carrying gifts. Each card mentioned an item or activity for his gift. One day it was his choice of what to do that day, go to the beach, shopping, show, etc. Another day it was a pedicure for both of us. A day of pampering. Liquor is very cheap in Mexico so one day he could buy his choice of one bottle for another gift. Each day I would give him a card. He loved it.

We spent the six days in Cozumel driving around the Island, going out for dinner, shopping, going to movies, lounging by the pool or on the beach. Nightlife in Cozumel is pretty much non existent but we found enough to do to keep us entertained.

Our favorite restaurant was The Thirsty Cougar. It's right in downtown Cozumel. They have the best chicken nachos ever. I go there every time I am in Cozumel.

Christmas Eve in our family is always spent at my house with a meal, and exchanging of gifts. Our traditional meal is steak and shrimp with all the fixin's. Matt and I were in Playa del Carmen for the last 3 Days of our trip, which included Christmas Eve and Christmas. Since that night was usually spent with my older son, my daughter-in-law Stephanie and my grandson Dylan, we were really missing them, so we Skyped with them from the restaurant.

Matt and I had our traditional steak and shrimp dinner. We always celebrated Christmas on Christmas Eve, so when Christmas day came around, it was all over but the crying. We would usually have a more traditional dinner on Christmas Day, but the gift-giving was over. Santa came and left gifts for the kids and they were excited, but when Santa stopped coming it was a pretty quiet day.

After dinner we went salsa dancing. We didn't know there was a CoCo Bongo in Playa Del Carmen or we would have gone. I learned it on my next trip the next year and went by myself and loved it.

Before our trip, we called and talked to Matt's friend in Mexico. Her name is Gloria and she teaches English in Mexico. Matt always helped her with English and she helped Matt with his Spanish when they were in college.

We talked to the class and told them we were spending the 12 Days of Christmas in Mexico. We explained there was a song of that name and we were just being silly by using that expression. We were on speaker phone and they asked if we would sing it. We said sure. So we sang it, and after the 6th day when we felt sure that they got the drift of the song, we stopped. They loved it. Can you believe that?

They asked Matt if he knew any rap songs and would he sing one. Matt knows all kinds of music and songs so he did his favorite. They thought it was awesome and said we were both good singers. They were easily impressed, although we weren't bad. Our family has always sang in choirs and groups and at home, all our lives.

I love Mexico, during the Twelve Days of Christmas or for seven days in the Spring. You always get a lot of bang for your buck. Ole'!

CHAPTER SEVEN
More to Las Vegas than the Strip

The best kept secrets of Las Vegas, in my opinion, are Red Rock Canyon and the Valley of Fire. Red Rock Canyon is approximately 24 miles from the Las Vegas Strip. It features a 13 Mile scenic drive, a visitor's center, and various look out spots when you can park, take pictures, hike on the trails, and climb the mountains.

There's a campground if you want to take a night away from the craziness of the strip. They have grills, picnic tables, trash collection, and water and toilets are also available. Bicycles are allowed on designated mountain bike trails.

There isn't any public transportation available to Red Rock Canyon, but if you rent a car it is easy to find. If you stay at a resort with a shuttle service they usually have a day trip that they take you there for a small charge. One of my Resorts did it for $5. You can't buy gas for that amount. What a deal.

Every time I go to Las Vegas I go to Red Rock Canyon. It's absolutely beautiful. Mountains in every direction. You can see a different terrain in every direction too.

Even though I spent a lot of time living in California, i.e. San Diego, Los Angeles, San Francisco, Sacramento and visiting many other cities there, I could still stand in Red Rock Canyon and be in awe of the natural beauty of the area.

After my first visit, whenever I go to Vegas, one day is always designated for a trip to Red Rock Canyon.

You can actually get a permit and have a wedding there. Weddings are allowed at Red Spring picnic area or Red Rock Overlook. It would be a lovely backdrop for a wedding. Before you ask, I'm not going to get married there.

If you are impressed with Red Rock Canyon, and I'm sure you will be, wait till you see the Valley of Fire. If you can tear yourself away from the casinos and shows another day, you need to drive 58 miles Northeast of Las Vegas, located in the Mojave Desert.

Valley of Fire is the oldest Nevada state park and was dedicated in 1935. It covers 35,000 Acres and is full of red stone formations that were formed from great shifting sand dunes during the age of the dinosaurs, more than a hundred and fifty million years ago.

Valley of Fire is a popular place to film and films like Transformers, Total Recall, and many others were filmed there. Star Trek Generations was filmed there and it was there that Captain Kirk fell to his death.

It's a nice drive for a day outing from Las Vegas. Take your camera, it's gorgeous. There are six top rated hiking trails. The first one being Fire Wave Hike; it's a 1.2 Mile Trail.

The second is the White Domes Hike, which is one mile Loop. The third is Mouse Tank Hike which is .75 miles out and back. The fourth is Rainbow Vista and Fire Canyon.

Overlook Hike and the Elephant Rock is next and the last is Petrified Logs, which is not a hike but it's worth seeing. Petroglyphs at Atlatl Rock is not a hike, but a set of metal stairs along the Whiteface to allow visitors to reach the petroglyphs.

Yeah the Vegas strip is fun, but venture out to these two places and you will see some of the most scenic places in the United States.

I went with my friend Jane. Jane and I met on a 10-day Southern Caribbean cruise and she lives in Las Vegas and works for the Forestry

Division of Nevada, and was an excellent tour guide. I can't wait to go again and spend more time at the Valley of Fire.

CHAPTER EIGHT

17 Days, 4 Countries with Only a Carry-On

Six months into my retirement, I decided to take a trip to Paris and London. I had waited long enough.

I had been on a cruise to the Mediterranean earlier in the year and then spent four days in Rome. I think Rome would have been more fun if traveling with someone, so I asked my dear friend and dance partner, Jon, if he would like to go with me.

He said he would go under one condition: He wanted to go to Ireland and Scotland too. I said sure, that would be awesome. Since the flight across the Atlantic was going to be the most expensive part of the trip, I agreed to add Dublin and Glasgow to our adventure.

We agreed we would each pay for our own flights, tours, meals and split the room cost. It was later that he suggested going with only a carry on so we could avoid the checked baggage and baggage claim. I was reluctant at first, but finally agreed. After all, this wasn't a cruise and there would be no formal night.

Initially I thought we would be taking trains from one country to the next. As it turned out, it was simpler and less expensive to fly. So I started booking flights allowing 4 days in each country starting with London. Next on my list of things to do was book hotels. I use hotels.com whenever possible. I booked hotels in four Cities, trying to get nights at around $100 per night. We would be splitting the cost, so $50 per night each would be great. Thinking we would use shuttles, taxis, buses, trains or subways from the airport to the hotels and back, that could be done upon arrival.

Now, the tourist attractions were next. I always had great luck with the double decker bus tours, so I went on Viator and booked one or two day tours in each city.

I usually do the complete tour once and stay on the bus, and the second time around hop-off and hop-on, depending on what I wanted to see up close and personal. These tours are usually great fun and you learn lots of trivia in the bargain. Maybe it is information of no great value, but fun just the same.

My son Matt took me to the airport and we picked up Jon in Little Rock on the way. Jon walked out the door with a carry-on and no personal bag. I said if you don't need a personal bag I can use it. So he went back in the house and got a small personal bag. Every little bit of packing room counts. If nothing else, I thought we could use it to pack souvenirs.

We arrived at Heathrow Airport in London and took a subway and a bus to our hotel. It was right in the center of London. That was pretty easy to do. We checked in, dropped off our luggage and took off to grab lunch and get on the tour bus. We had lunch at a beautiful bakery on a main thoroughfare and caught our tour bus down the street.

We were going to Buckingham Palace! It looked just like in the pictures and on TV. We took tons of pictures. We went to the London Bridge, the Tower Bridge (which I always thought was the London Bridge), Big Ben, and rode the London Eye, a 440 foot ferris wheel, much like the High Roller in Las Vegas only about 100 feet shorter.

We went across The Westminster Bridge and took pictures of and then from the bridge, which is very close to the London Eye. We were on that bridge a week before the attack that injured more than 50 people in March of 2017.

Our stops in Dublin and Glasgow were fun and interesting but my favorite city was Paris. We had breakfast at a lovely restaurant close to our hotel; it was a huge breakfast and would tide us over for the majority of the day.

We took the train into the city where we would see the Eiffel Tower. When I first got a glimpse of the Eiffel Tower I was thrilled beyond words. It was raining, we purchased umbrellas from street vendors and started walking towards the tower. I was really there!

There were only about 15 people ahead of us in line. Picking a rainy day had its advantages. It wasn't long before we were in a large elevator with about 15 other tourists and the tour guide. I took pictures from the elevator on the way up. It was fascinating to see the inner parts of the elevator shaft and the tower. We stopped at the observation deck and looked at the view from all available angles and took tons of pictures. We visited the gift shop and picked up postcards, magnets, and Matt's precious mug.

We took the double decker bus tour after our Tower visit and would pass the Eiffel Tower a few times during the tour.

We spent our days touring and experiencing the local restaurants and pubs. It was wonderful!

After our allotted four days we flew to Dublin, Ireland. In addition to local bus tours, we purchased tickets on tour buses to places like the Cliffs of Moher. The Sea Cliffs there range from 393 to 700 ft. The Cliffs rank among the most visited tourist sites in Ireland, with around 1.5 million visitors per year. It was about a 3-hour drive on a tour bus from Dublin, 267 km or 165 miles. I didn't have a clue how far 267 kilometers would be. It was a beautiful drive on freeways and small winding country roads with lots of roundabouts. It was worth every second of the drive.

When we first arrived, it was foggy, so the pictures I took of the cliffs weren't the greatest. I went in the visitor center, purchased postcards, a magnet for Tammy, and I took "pictures of pictures" in case the fog didn't lift. We walked back to the cliffs and voila! The fog had Lifted! I was able to take pictures, selfies, and pose for Jon to take my picture and me to take his. I had been on a bus for 3 hours and walked around in the fog for an hour by then. Can you say frizzy and wilted hair? Well I took pics anyway, proof I was really there.

On the trip back to Dublin, we stopped at a lovely little village and ate lunch at a local pub. They were serving Irish stew, drinks, and sandwiches in record time. Lots of buses stop there before heading back to the other cities across Ireland.

We drove by the Guiness Brewery in Dublin several times. I said Guinness would turn over in his grave because instead of ordering a Guinness with my delicious dinner of Lamb Chops, I ordered a Bud light at a local pub.

The people in Ireland, as well as Scotland, were very friendly. Always willing to give you directions or answer questions. The whole trip was like a dream. I wanted to go to these places for years and I was finally there! I counted my blessings every day of the trip. When I think about it now, I still can't believe it.

Having just said how "dreamlike" it all was, I always wanted to share these experiences with someone very special, but I figured I had waited long enough. I was going if I had to go alone. Jon was the perfect travel companion. Always the gentleman and willing to go almost anywhere.

Another of our side trips included a day in Scotland. We took the 58 mile ride on the train. We went to Edinburgh Castle to see the Crown Jewels in the Scotland capital city of Edinburgh. On another day we took a double decker bus tour of Glasgow.

You're probably wondering if we did laundry or wore dirty clothes. No to both of those questions. We packed jeans (jeans and leggings for me) sweaters, turtlenecks, and I packed a pair New Balance tennis shoes. I wore a pair of boots, and we both wore hooded waterproof jackets on the trip to London. You can roll up underwear to practically nothing so that wasn't a problem. You're allowed one personal bag so I took advantage of that also to pack personal items.

CHAPTER NINE

Real Women Don't Pay Full Price!

I'm not one to clip coupons but I'm always looking for a bargain. My motto: Real women don't pay full price. With very few exceptions, I stick to this rule. I did pay full price at Dillard's for a dress to wear to my son's wedding, but it was really beautiful and it was a special occasion.

I'm acquainted with every sale rack in the city. I have used Groupons when out of town for tours, massages, pedicures, dinners, anything to get more bang for my buck.

When at home I use Groupons for oil changes, shows and events, massages, dinners at local restaurants, luggage, sheets, laptops, gifts, and concerts.

When I was in Las Vegas I bought a day tour on Groupon to the Grand Canyon for $99. I saved $100 on that purchase. When I was in Toronto Canada, I purchased an all-day tour to Niagara Falls and that trip was half price too.

Every city I go to, I use a Groupon to get a massage. A little bit of heaven on a budget. The massages are usually half price plus tip. $65 to $90 might not be in my budget but $30-$45 sure is. It's all prepaid so the only out-of-pocket expense is a $10 or $15 tip at the time of service.

I use Groupons at local restaurants in the cities that I travel to. It is usually 50% off the total tab and I get to experience places that aren't in my budget at full price.

I've passed this way of buying on to my youngest son and he's always finding bargains. I think I created a monster sometimes, because he is something of a shopaholic. Sorry Matt. Don't get me wrong I think it's great that he looks for bargains and saves money.

When Matt was 21 he was a companion for a young man with Autism. His job was to take this young man to the gym, guitar lessons, movies, concerts, out to dinner, etc. Not a bad gig really. He got paid to have fun! He told me he was going to accompany this young man to Hot Springs, AR, about an hour away, for a week and stay at his mom's lake house. I thought that would be a cool experience.

The truth was, as I was told 9 months after the fact, Matt and two of his college friends from England drove to Las Vegas! Matt was dying to tell me, but knew I would try to talk him out of it. Nine months later, he just couldn't keep the secret any longer so he finally fessed up. He said he took his brand new car and they drove straight through from Little Rock to Las Vegas, taking turns at the wheel.

Just to soften the blow, he explained how they got a cheap hotel deal from one of the casino coupons and used Groupon to do club crawls and concerts. That made me feel so much better... Not! Oh my God, I could have killed him! All those miles in a brand new car all the way across the country!

He's still breathing and walking, so I got over being upset. I was proud of him for saving money, after I got over being mad. Kids! You gotta love em!

One of my sweeter stories of Matt and Groupon is when he asked me at the beginning of my retirement what color luggage I would like if I got new luggage. My luggage at the time was black and I would put curly ribbons on the handle so I could spot it easily at baggage claim.

I told him I had good luggage, but if I were to buy more it would be light blue or hot pink. Again, so I could spot it easily.

When I returned from my first trip of retirement, there was a three piece set of rolling luggage in a beautiful turquoise color sitting in my living room, waiting on me. He bought it on Groupon for my "birthday" (it was three months before my birthday). So sweet. Matt was working at the college police department as a dispatcher and working part time as a bartender at the time; he didn't make a lot of money, so that made it even sweeter.

I know I've shared many stories about my kids, but they have been "my life". I would kiddingly refer to them as my "pride and joy". But they really were, and still are.

While we're on the subject of saving money you won't believe how much bang-for-your-buck you get in Mexico. I've visited Puerto Vallarta several times, Mazatlan, Cabo San Lucas, Cancun, Cozumel and Playa Del Carmen. You don't need a Groupon there. You can get a massage for $20 to $40 an hour. I usually splurge and get two in a week.

Compared to the U.S., the restaurants are really cheap, even at the finer restaurants. I've seriously considered moving there. I've met couples that move there during retirement and love it. I think it would be more attractive if I wasn't single though.

Even without using money from bribes given to me from resorts, doing everything I want to do is very reasonable. I stay at beautiful resorts, dine out every meal, get massages, take tours, venture out on a city bus, sometimes ending up where there were horses and chickens on a dirt road. I feel perfectly safe and meet the nicest people on all my adventures.

People in the states are always asking me "Aren't you afraid?" I just tell them the truth: No! You can get killed in Little Rock. You just don't go in bad areas, dark side streets, etc.

You can usually find someone that speaks English, especially in retail shops, restaurants, and hotels. The people are friendly and will help you with directions.

I've even had dates in many of the cities in Mexico. Men there seem to be attracted to blondes.

Shopping in Mexico is so much fun. I have a collection of pewter plates, platters, and bowls that were purchased at 50% off in Cozumel. I go to the same shop on every visit.

Mexico is a great place to buy cowboy boots at bargain prices. I've purchased eight pair of boots in the last few years. One of my favorite pair is a bright red pair I purchased at a mall in Cabo San Lucas. They started out at $450 US Dollars and after some negotiating I ended up getting them for $150 US dollars. I was happy, they were happy. What a deal!

CHAPTER TEN

My Dream Cruise – I Can't Miss My Ship!

I always wanted to sail the Mediterranean. The cruise prices were reasonable enough, but the flight over to Barcelona and back to the United States was way over my budget. The cost was anywhere from $1700 to $1800. Ouch!

It's not cheap to fly anywhere out of Little Rock like it is from one of the hubs like New York, Los Angeles, Dallas, Chicago, or Atlanta. So, I continued to look. I kept searching on different flight brokers and finally found a flight on CheapOAir. Yes, I said CheapOAir. It was a United Airlines flight to Barcelona with a change of planes in Toronto for less than a thousand dollars. $907 to be exact.

I had already been looking for a cruise that didn't have a single-cruiser supplement on Vacations to Go. There was a 12 day Mediterranean Cruise on the Holland America cruise line for less than a thousand dollars. Bingo! I found my cruise.

While I was online ready to book the cruise, I called CheapOAir and made sure the flight I wanted was available. It was, so I booked the cruise and flight. I was going to the Mediterranean!

While I was booking the flight I thought "As long as I am paying all that airfare, I might as well include a side trip to Rome after my cruise." So I made my return five days after my cruise, giving me four days in Rome! Wow! I was so excited.

I then started looking on Hotels.com for a hotel in Rome. I got a reasonable rate for four nights. I was all set. This was my first big trip after retirement.

I left Little Rock on July 10th and arrived in Barcelona on July 11th. I boarded the ship and, the next day was spent entirely at sea. The following days we were in Cadiz, then Alicante, Malaga, in Spain. Then we went to Gibraltar and Palma de Mallorca, Spain. We ended the third leg with another day at sea, Marseille and Calvi Corsica in France, Monte Carlo in Monaco, and Florence and Pisa in Italy. A day in each city and four days in Rome after the cruise. Then, back home to the United States July 28th.

I had booked and paid in advance for double decker bus tours. I've had the best experiences on these tours in cities in the U.S. so I knew what they would be like. You can get a great overview of the city. These tours range from $25 - $30. I usually meet people on these tours and sometimes we will finish up the day touring together.

I met a sweet, pretty, young lady named Megan in Marseille, France. We struck up a conversation on the bus and decided to take in some of the sights together. She was from the U.S. and was a nanny for a couple in France while she was on a break between graduation from a college in Georgia and going to Vietnam to teach English on a six month assignment. Megan was so precious, I wanted to bring her home with me to meet my son. We are still Facebook friends.

I was on a corner in Monte Carlo, Monaco and a beautiful young lady by the name of Ini asked if I would take her picture in front of the Casino Monte Carlo. This was the Casino you see in the James Bond movie with Pierce Brosnan. I took her picture and then we took pictures of each other at various locations. We decided to have lunch, go to the casino, and just walk around Monte Carlo.

At the time, Ini worked for the Radisson Hotel in Chisinau, Moldova. Ini and I are still Facebook friends. Ini was not only beautiful, but was the sweetest young lady. Another one I wanted to bring home to my son. She was so considerate, and at the end of the day, she wouldn't leave me till I was on my bus to return to my ship. Ini was taking the train back to her home.

At my first stop in Aliante, Spain, I went to McDonalds. You can get free wifi at McDonalds everywhere, so it was one of my favorite spots to email and stay in touch with my kids. I met the sweetest couple from England. Beverly and Adrian. We struck up a conversation and probably spent an hour visiting. They go to Spain a couple of times a year. Bev is a school teacher and Adrian is in the automotive repair industry. They love to travel and it was fun sharing stories. We still stay in touch by email and talk about our travels.

The cruise ship was the MS Rotterdam. All the names of the Holland America ships end in dam. The Holland America line is a British owned cruise line and is a subsidiary of Carnival Corporation. The ships are named things like Rotterdam, Amsterdam, Noordam, Westerdam, etc. Affectionately referred to as the Dam ships. I bought my son a mug for his collection with all the Dam ships names on it.

We had approximately 300 Australians on board. My favorite Australian was Zillah. She was a nail salon owner from Brisbane, Queensland, Australia. I met Zillah on a roll call before the cruise but it took a day or two to finally connect and meet in person. I was on the pool deck and saw this exotic looking, gorgeous woman. Lovely hair, beautiful nails (of course), and a personality that wouldn't quit. It had to be Zillah. I introduced myself. I don't know if it was mutual or not but I liked her immediately.

We were both single and both attended events for solo travelers. Holland America did a great job of getting solo travelers together. We had a luncheon first, happy hour get togethers, cocktail parties, etc. We had a group of about 25 that attended. On other cruise lines I am usually one of two people that show up for those type of events.

This group was lots of fun and Zillah and I are still Facebook friends. Zillah was so much fun and taught me so many Australian expressions… and of course I loved her accent.

A group of us would meet on the pool deck and get some sun, laugh, talk, etc. I wish Arkansas wasn't so far from Australia; I would love to see her again.

Holland America is a very classy line without being out of sight expense wise. Their rooms are basically the same as Carnival and Royal Caribbean or Norwegian.

Their casual dining is lovely. They actually have orchids in the casual dining and servers are there to serve drinks or refills. The buffet is still served and you don't have to go from line to line to get a complete meal. Two and a half years ago you could even get Eggs Benedict with all the fixings from room service. It was on a covered plate warmer. It was all fresh and delicious.

The entertainment was wonderful. We actually had a concert pianist for the show one night. He was fantastic. Not everyone's taste, but I loved it. The only things I missed on that cruise was the disco (what's disco?) and the comedy club.

They did have an area off the promenade called Lincoln Center and there were daily performances of a string quartet. Violins, Viola, Cello, and sometimes accompanied by piano. In another area there was a pianist playing classical music and popular tunes.

Don't expect to see participation in crazy deck games. It won't happen. This cruise line caters to an older more settled group than the "Fun Ships". Not that it is bad, just different.

Dinners are formal and lovely. Dine with the same people and have the same wait staff for the entire cruise. Love the dining! I still stay in contact with dining companions through email and Facebook.

I was pleasantly surprised with the ports. They weren't primitive like some in the Caribbean, Eastern or Western. Some of the most beautiful architecture in the world.

Our stop in Livorno, Italy was the port where we took a bus to go to Pisa. I was so excited! Matt and I built a model of The Leaning Tower of Pisa when he was in elementary school. Now I was going to see it in person! How cool is that?

It was about a thirty minute bus ride, and I sat on the front seat of the bus and had a great view of the countryside. I thought I would see the Leaning Tower in the distance when approaching, but I didn't.

We parked with about twenty five other buses and walked a few blocks through a neighborhood to get to the fenced in square that housed the Leaning Tower of Pisa, The Putti Fountain, Pisa Cathedral and Piazza de Miracoli (Square of Miracles) in Pisa, Tuscany, Central Italy.

People were all over the place taking pictures, posing as if the Tower of Pisa was in their hand. Kind of a fair-like atmosphere. There were shops and restaurants adjacent to the square with sidewalk or outside dining. I stopped at one of the sidewalk cafes and had a cold drink and, as I sat there, I had a view of the Tower.

When leaving I stopped at a couple of vendors to get souvenirs and a magnet for my friend Tammy.

I was heading back to the buses, or so I thought. I was following the crowd when things weren't looking familiar and I only had a little over thirty minutes to get to the bus. I couldn't miss the bus!

I stopped in a local barber shop to see if they could direct me. Not much English was spoken there. I went in a local pub and luckily there was a man in there from Pisa, but he lived in New York and was there visiting family. He said "I will take you there". Relieved, I followed him outside. I thought he meant he would drive me there. He meant he would "walk" me back. I was starting to panic, on the inside, but followed him. Sure enough, we came up to the bus parking lot. Thank you Lord!

Now… which bus is mine? I walked through the buses till I recognized my bus driver. Thank God I had sat up front and had a good idea of who to look for. The bus was idling when I got to the door and a young man was sitting in my seat. (No it didn't have my name on it.)

I was going to walk to the back of the bus when the young man said, "No, you can have your seat." Wasn't that nice?

I took my seat, my heart still racing from rushing to find my bus. We had an uneventful ride back to Livorno and I had plenty of time to walk around and see the little town before returning to the ship. How do you spell relief? If you haven't ever cruised before, YOU DO NOT WANT TO BE LATE RETURNING TO THE SHIP UNLESS YOU WANT TO GET LEFT BEHIND!

I didn't study the cities or ports I was going to visit so I was pleasantly surprised at what most ports had to offer. The only port I was excited about beforehand was Pisa.

When we stopped at Gibraltar in the UK Territory I had no idea I was going to see or go to the Rock of Gibraltar! I just starting walking to the quaint little town from the port. The closer I got to town I started to see shops and restaurants and signs about going to the Rock.

I saw a huge line of people waiting to buy tickets for a Tram. Then I saw some vans and men asking people if they wanted to take a van to the top of the Rock. I wasn't crazy about hanging from a cable in a cable car, so I said I would like to take a van. The rock's highest point is 1,398 feet. Did I ever mention I was afraid of heights? I had to go to an ATM on the property and get cash. I don't remember if it was Euros or Pounds but I got what I needed from the ATM. We were on our way up the small winding road up the mountain.

I was with a family, not sure where they were from. I'm sure I knew at the time, though. I rarely meet a stranger.

When we got to our first stop, we went in some caves and when we got back outside we were greeted by lots of little, and also not so little, monkeys. We were told not to pet or feed them. They were trying to get in our van. We continued up the one lane winding road to the top.

It was very windy and had an amazing view of the city, the port, and our ship, and from one point you can see both continents of Africa and Europe. The point that we could see both countries was a stop on the south side two thirds up the Rock.

You can also see the International Gibraltar Airport from the top of the Rock. There is actually a busy four lane road that crosses the landing strip. If the road cannot be cleared when the plane is about 3 miles out, the landing will be diverted. It is one of the most interesting airports in the world, but very safe.

The town offered lots of shopping and I toured the shops and stopped for an ice cream cone and did some "people watching" before returning to the ship.

I'm not going to bore you to death with every stop we made on that cruise, but all the stops or ports were amazing and I was having the time of my life.

After the cruise ended, I took a shuttle bus to Rome. We disembarked in Civitavecchia (try saying that fast three times) and it took approximately an hour and half to get to Rome.

We were dropped at the city center and then took turns getting a taxi with all our luggage from a 12 day cruise. Finally getting a taxi, I was on my way to my hotel.

I booked my hotel online, so I wasn't sure what to expect. I saw pictures, but that can sometimes be misleading. I didn't have a clue where it was or how convenient it would be to get into town each day. We drove for about 30 minutes at a rate of 50 Euros. At the exchange rate now, it would be $56.69 in US Dollars. I was looking around and all I saw was graffitti. Not feeling too good about the neighborhood, I told the driver I needed to go back in the city and find a hotel.

He told me he had a friend (Max) that owned a bed and breakfast and he would call and see if he had any vacancies if I wanted. I asked, "Is it clean?" and "Would I have my own bathroom?" He said yes to both questions so I told him to make the call. He called his friend Max and was told he had a vacancy and would meet me there at 3 p.m.

It was probably around 2 p.m. at the time. So we were off to find the B&B. By the time we got there, the meter was up to 100 Euros or approx $113.00. Ouch!

My first day in Rome and I had spent over a hundred bucks and hadn't even gotten to my hotel. Not to mention my other hotel was prepaid, so that money was lost too.

The taxi driver dropped me off in a neighborhood of high rise buildings, right in front of a little Italian (what else?) restaurant. The driver told the lady from the restaurant I was going to meet Max.

This very sweet lady didn't speak english other than a word or two. She said "sit" and offered me a chair at a table with two chairs in front of her (closed) restaurant. I sat. She brought out a glass and a bottle of water. By then I was in tears. She got a kleenex and started wiping my tears and that made me cry even more. I was tired and so frustrated. I could have used a drink. A few minutes later Max walked up.

Luckily, Max spoke English. It was broken English, but we could communicate. He said he would take me to his B&B, which was next door. He told me he was on the 4th floor. I thought things were looking up, and then realized it was the 4th floor! Then I looked at all my luggage. He said "I help." I could just see us walking up four flights of stairs with all that luggage. Three bags. Then he said "We have lift." Another sigh of relief. I then realized that he probably didn't accept credit cards. I gave all my cash to the taxi driver. I told Max that and he said not to worry, he would take me the next day to get cash from an ATM.

God was watching out for me. This sweet man was going to let me stay without paying him up front. So we went next door, he used a key to get in the building. It was a world war two building, beautiful marble floors and a tiny elevator that had a folding metal gate over the opening.

By the time we got my luggage in and we got in, we were standing face to face, very close. Very cozy. We started up, then we got out on the fourth floor. Max used another key to get in the apartment. It was a four bedroom apartment. We were in a foyer where he had the wifi password posted and there was a lovely antique bookcase and desk. We went down the hall and he used a third key to get into my room. I was thinking "At least it is secure." He showed me the room, how to turn on the AC with the remote, the bathroom, etc. He said when I left the room to please turn off the air, but while I was in the room I could turn it as high as I wanted. The AC unit was mounted about eight feet up on the wall. Oh well, I had a remote.

He asked what time I would like to have breakfast. Not sure what would be convenient for him I said, how about 9:30 a.m.? He said fine and he would be back then.

I was the only tennant at the time and he lived in a different location. So I had this huge apartment to myself.

Before he left he gave me directions to the bus stop and told me Bus 13 would get me to town, about two miles away and to take it back when returning to the B&B.

I had a more detailed look around the room. It had a mural on one wall, a queen size bed, a couple of upholstered chairs, a couple of end tables, and a clock. All the comforts any hotel would offer, but with an "old charm". I didn't have to stay at a Marriott or Hilton. I was okay.

I decided to wash my face and put on fresh make-up. I was a mess after crying downstairs.

I also needed to use the restroom after riding a bus, taking a taxi and basically traveling from early that morning. One thing Max didn't show me was how to flush the toilet. That should have been a no brainer, right? Well, it wasn't.

I started looking around and couldn't find a handle anywhere. I saw a sprayer connected by a metal flexible pipe next to the toilet. I sprayed it in the toilet. Nothing happened. I kept looking. There was a cord hanging from an unusual looking box over the toilet up high. At first I was afraid to pull the cord; I didn't know if I would be summoning help or what. I finally decided "what the heck" and I pulled the cord. The toilet flushed. Another "Thank God" moment.

I gathered my three keys, purse, debit and credit card, phone, and tablet and took off for my first adventure in Rome. I had another one of those moments where I needed to pinch myself. I was in ROME!

I walked down the street to the corner and turned right and sure enough, just like Max described, there was was a sign indicating it was a bus stop. So far, so good.

It was only a few minutes and a bus stopped. I got on the bus and tried to pay the driver. He pointed toward a machine about mid way back on the bus. So I go to the machine. I couldn't figure out what to do. It appeared that I needed to have a ticket or card, that I didn't have. I should have purchased one at a machine before getting on the bus. So my first bus ride was free…

I rode a couple of miles and it appeared I was getting to a tourist area so I got off the bus and walked. It was amazing. Looking around at all the ancient buildings. Wow.

One of the first things I saw was the Il Vittoriano in Piazza Venezia. Lots of tourists were on the steps and various places in and around the building, trying to get that perfect picture. I was among them.

It is a central part of the city, at least I thought it was. I would see it many more times in the next four days.

I was ready for something to eat so I stopped at a sidewalk cafe; what else would I do? When in Rome! I ordered a pizza and a coke. It was delicious! Maybe that was because I hadn't eaten since early that morning. I ate half of it and took the rest of it back to my B&B and put it in the fridge. I threw it away the next day. No more doggie bags.

I decided to just walk around and take my tour the next day when I could get an earlier start. When it got dark and I was getting tired, I started looking for a bus to take me back to my B&B.

Not having much luck, I decided to take a taxi. I waited till I got in familiar territory, so I wouldn't encounter another $100 taxi ride. I saw a taxi in front of a deli. I went in the deli and a gentleman was walking out. I asked if he was a taxi driver. He said yes. I asked if that was his taxi in front of the deli. He replied yes again. I then asked if he could take me to the place on a business card I showed him. He again said yes. Relief.

We went to his taxi and he called the number on the card. I understood the words American and Blonde. He was talking to Max, asking directions. It turned out to be only a $10 taxi ride.

We visited a little on the way and I learned his name was Roberto. When he stopped at my building, he asked if I would like to go and have a drink. I immediately answered yes. That was just what I wanted. A drink!

I asked if I could sit up front and I moved to the front seat. He took me to a really nice place about three blocks away. It was a restaurant/bar. We ordered drinks, talked, laughed, took selfies and then he took me back to my B&B.

He asked if I had a ride to the airport when leaving Rome. I said not yet. He said he would take me. It was a 48 Euro fare. I said "Okay, but you have to be at my B&B at 10 a.m. on Tuesday or I would call someone else." He assured me he would be there.

The next morning, Max arrived at the B&B and knocked on my door. He was there to prepare my breakfast. I went to the kitchen with him, and he showed me what he had for breakfast items.

There were various cereals, sweet rolls, coffee, juice, milk. I chose a sweet roll and drank the diet coke I had saved from the night before. We had a lovely visit.

After breakfast Max walked me to a store in the neighborhood that had, not only an ATM, but a place where I could buy a bus ticket that would be valid for 4 days. No more "free" bus rides. I felt guilty about the first ride without paying. Though, the more I observed over the next few days, there were a lot of people that took "free" rides.

Max walked me back to the B&B and I took off for the bus stop. I got off at the same stop I had the day before and I found the Double Decker Bus Tours and used my prepaid voucher for a 48 hour tour.

The real tour began and I took tons of pictures as well as sitting quietly in awe of all I was seeing. It seemed we would pass the Colosseum several times in a tour while going to other places of interest. Later, I would tire of seeing the Colosseum. "Not again."

We saw the Pantheon, The Trevi Fountain, The Piazza Venezia, and so many other beautiful and historical sights, to include the Vatican.

After my 48 hour pass on the double decker bus expired I started taking the city buses. I would pick a bus, ride it to the end of its route and ride it back. I was surprised to see there were no houses. There were small and large buildings that housed apartments and condos, but no houses.

The sad thing I saw was graffitti. All over the place. I'm not talking about artistic type graffitti, because a lot of that is beautiful. I'm talking about graffitti you would relate to vandalism. Such a beautiful city had been marked up with it! Thank goodness none of the historical or famous monuments or structures were touched.

While I was having lunch, I saw an advertisement for The Three Tenors. They were appearing at a cathedral downtown and I decided to go that evening.

I went back to my B&B, showered, put on fresh make-up, did my hair, and put on a classy looking black jumpsuit, heels, jewelry, and perfume. I took off for the bus stop. The bus was packed. I would venture to say I was the best smelling, if not the best looking person on the bus. I don't think average European people put as much emphasis on "smelling good" as we Americans do. No offense intended. Just fact.

I wasn't sure which stop to get off and asked a young man, probably in his thirties, if he spoke English. He was a tourist from Paris.

He asked if he could help me. When I told him where I was attempting to go, he immediately took his smart phone out and looked it up and then gave me directions. He was telling me to go about so many meters and it would be on the right and I couldn't miss it. It was supposed to be a huge cathedral, so I thought even though I didn't know how many "meters" that was, or how far it was, I would just walk till I found it. He actually got off the bus with me to make sure I was headed in the right direction.

I found it, just as he said I would. It was a beautiful cathedral and I was pleasantly surprised that the concert was free! The acoustics were wonderful and I thoroughly enjoyed the concert even though it was a choir from Vienna, not the Three Tenors.

After the concert I started to look for a place to have a late dinner. I spotted a beautiful hotel and was directed to a lovely courtyard in the center of the hotel. Dinner was great, and the waiter was charming. They all seemed to be very professional and gracious.

Now to the task of finding my B&B. I crossed the street in front of the hotel and waited for a bus. Bus 13 came along and I took it. After a few miles, I recognized the restaurant/bar that was in the neighborhood of my B&B so I got off the bus. I figured I could find my home away from home from there.

I was walking among the high rise apartment buildings. The streets were lined with small European cars at that time of night. I could hear family's talking from the open windows. I asked directions once from a couple that passed me on the street. Then I saw my building!

The restaurant next door was crowded. Tables and chairs were set up outside and it was a lively group of customers. I didn't stop, but let myself in my building and went up on the open-air elevator to my room.

I had another pleasant day in Rome and, although it was fairly late at night and the sidewalks were empty except for the couple I passed, I felt perfectly safe.

On the day I was to fly home, Roberto, my taxi driver, showed up before 10 a.m., just as he promised. Max helped me carry my luggage downstairs, and I took pictures with him and the nice lady next door and thanked her and Max for being so kind, and took off to the airport with Roberto.

I sat in the front seat and Roberto and I talked about staying in touch. I asked if he had Facebook or email. He said he didn't have either, but he had a phone. I don't have an international calling plan, so we left it at that.

Roberto asked if I would like to stop for coffee. I said yes, but would like a diet coke instead. We stopped at a little coffee shop and visited some more.

We got to the airport in plenty of time for me to catch my flight. He got out to help me with my luggage and as we were saying goodbye, he stepped closer to me and just planted a very passionate kiss on me. We separated, and then he kissed me again! Wow!

That's my luck. I meet a good-looking man that I am attracted to and he lives in Rome! Well, it put a smile on my face and gave me something to smile about on the way home. A sweet memory of my last day in Rome.

CHAPTER ELEVEN
That's Your Uniform?

Orlando was the trip or adventure I planned for May 2018. I booked a two-bedroom, two-bath condo in Kissimmee, Florida.

I was hoping my nephew in Tampa might drive up and spend the weekend and go to Disney with me. That didn't happen; he got deployed and was out of the country for a couple of months. So I had a lovely two bedroom two bath condo to myself for $349.

I had stayed at this resort when I took my son, his wife, and my grandson on an 11-day Disney trip before and knew it had all the comforts of home plus two pools, two hot tubs, clubhouse, basketball court, etc.

I arrived at the airport and attempted to pick up my rental car. I had booked a new, red Mustang. It took forever to get my car and when I got to it, there were no keys in it. My car was unlocked, so I put my luggage in my car and I went to the counter in the parking garage.

Another line, after just waiting 45 minutes in line in the terminal. Oh my God. I was not a happy camper. I walked up to a (no line) window and told the lady, the keys were not in my car. She finally got an employee to find the keys and help me. I was then headed to my resort.

I made it to my resort, checked in and went to my unit. Only then did I find out it was on the second floor. No elevator! Lesson One: Ask for ground floor when traveling alone.

After getting part of my luggage upstairs, I took off to grab something to eat and pick up some things to have in the condo.

I was familiar with the area, so I knew there were fast food restaurants and stores close by. It was around 7 p.m. by then. I found a Dollar Tree and picked up soft drinks, some snacks, and a few breakfast items in case I didn't want to drive out of the complex first thing in the mornings.

The first morning, I wanted to relax by the pool, sit in the hot tub, and just start my vacation. A short time after noon, I decided to get dressed and go out for lunch.

I was driving along, at the posted speed, and saw two Mexican restaurants on the opposite side of the road. I made a u-turn. It was a legal turn, so no worries. I picked one of the restaurants at a small strip mall and went in, was seated, and was looking over the menu.

A man walked up to my table. If you couldn't tell where this is going, he was wearing short cargo pants, a golf shirt, a tactical vest, gun, and belt with the radio, cuffs, etc. He showed me his badge, told me he was with the Sheriff's Department, and asked if I would step outside with him.

It was broad daylight and he had a badge, so I said okay. We stepped outside and he pointed to my rental car, the red Mustang, and asked if that was my vehicle. I said, "It's my rental car."

He then said it had been reported stolen. You can imagine my alarm and shock. I told him all my paperwork was at my resort and that I didn't like papers and such cluttering up the vehicle.

I then remembered my confirmation from the rental agency was on my mini Ipad. I proceeded to find this in my email. Proof I had rented, not stolen, the vehicle.

There were three unmarked sheriff's vehicles and two marked vehicles and five sheriff's department personnel surrounding me and my rented Mustang.

They were all in civilian clothes, tactical vests, guns, etc. I asked, "Is this the way you always dress?" One young officer said, "This is Florida". I asked, "Are you going to cuff me?" The same young officer said, "No, we might taze you though." The Sergeant was talking to his dispatcher and they were talking to the rental agency.

While all this was going on I said, "I need a picture of all this." I was going to take a selfie with two of the officers and the officer that had been doing most of the talking to me said, "Here, we'll have one of the other officers take the picture." So we posed for a picture, me between two officers. All smiling.

Then I realized the marked sheriff's cars were not in the picture. I said, "We need another picture with the patrol cars in the background." So we all moved and posed for another picture.

Then I said "I need a picture of all of you together." So they lined up and I took that picture.

The same officer I'd been talking to said "You know you lost us when we were following you? All five of us. Now that's doing something." I replied "I didn't know you were behind me, much less following me." It was hilarious.

They told me of their conversations, that I didn't look like a car thief, etc. These guys were so nice. I was thinking this will be a story to tell the folks back home.

It took about an hour to get the situation all cleared up. I told the officers that I knew they couldn't have a drink while on duty, but I would be happy to buy them all a cup of coffee or a soft drink after we got all this straightened out. They thanked me but didn't take me up on my offer. They were still on duty. They all got in their vehicles except for the sergeant.

He told me he wasn't afraid that I would run out the back door and, if I wanted to go back to the restaurant, he would come in and tell me when all of the confusion was straightened out.

The rental car company had apparently not notified the authorities that the late rental car had been returned and was not really stolen. The sergeant said he didn't want me to get stopped again so he wanted the records to be right.

I've never had such a sweet, considerate, encounter with law enforcement, and I am a fan of cops, having had police officers in my immediate, as well as extended, family. They deserve all the respect they can get.

I went back in the Mexican restaurant and was eating my lunch and drinking a cold beer. The Mariachi band was singing my favorite song to me at my table. "Besame Mucho". The sergeant stuck his head in the door, and gave me a thumbs up and left.

I felt like I just had one of those Lucy moments. My little sister Terri Lynne and I seem to have those kind of situations like on "I Love Lucy" quite often. We call them Lucy moments.

After all the excitement died down I decided to drive to St.Petersburg and see one of my "adopted kids". My son Matt's childhood friend Dustin, and "across-the-street neighbor", had moved there and got married to a beautiful redhead, Christin. The timing was perfect for me because they had just signed papers on their new home. We went to a lovely restaurant across from the beach to have dinner and celebrate.

After dinner, we went across the street to the beach to watch the sunset and take pictures. The visit was short but very sweet. Dustin has always been like a big brother to Matt and the sweetest influence. He's like one of my kids.

I drove back to Orlando that night. No other stops from the Sheriff's office.

The next day I wanted to go to the beach, after getting just a taste of it at Dustin and Christin's. I decided on Cocoa Beach. Matt and I had gone there years ago on our Disney trip. It was a beautiful day and, after a quick lunch when arriving in Cocoa Beach, I found a parking lot with public beach access and gathered my things and settled in for the afternoon.

It was a beautiful day, there was a nice breeze and the sound of the surf was just what I needed. I hated to leave, but the sun was setting and I wanted to get back before it was too late. I still had to make a stop at a souvenir shop for a magnet for Tammy and a mug for Matt.

On the way back to Orlando, I saw the most beautiful sunset. I pulled over to the side of the road to take pictures so I could text them to my kids and friends.

The next day I laid out by the pool and went for my usual massage that afternoon. Thanks to Groupon, I had an hour of complete relaxation. I found a nice steakhouse restaurant and went there for dinner that evening.

I was asked to tour a sister property and my bribe was a gift card for $100. The property was near the Orlando Eye, so I decided to go. I went and had brunch and listened to a brief sales pitch.

While in Orlando, I decided to ride The Orlando Eye. It's a 400 foot tall Ferris Wheel. I sort of made it a thing to do, when there was an enclosed ferris wheel in the city I was visiting, to ride on it. Las Vegas, London, and now Orlando. I did this one alone and had a capsule or car all to myself.

The view from the top was beautiful. I took pictures, of course, and just enjoyed the ride. Each capsule has a capacity of 15 passengers and it takes 20 minutes to complete the ride.

I spent the remainder of my time in Florida relaxing by the pool, dining out, and just enjoying the resort.

The last day, I went to the pool in the morning, then packed my "stolen car" and took it back to the airport in the afternoon, before returning to Little Rock.

CHAPTER TWELVE

Who Says People in New York/New Jersey Aren't Friendly?

I had visited New York many times over the years. I worked for MetLife for a couple of years and our home office was in Manhattan. I was a Human Resource Specialist.

With a company that large, when you work in HR, they want you to be trained at the Home Office before taking on large projects that dealt with Equal Employment Opportunity or Affirmative Action Plans, new insurance plans, etc. This involved a trip to Manhattan.

Tough duty, I know. As much as I loved to travel, this was not something I dreaded. I was picked up and returned to the airport in a stretch limousine, staying in beautiful hotels, dined on an expense account, and had plenty of free time to see the city.

My first trip to Manhattan for Metlife in 1993 was also my first trip to New York. My first experience in taking Double Decker Bus Tours was to take an Upper Manhattan and Lower Manhattan tour.

I got to see things I had seen in movies and on television my whole life. It was wonderful.

My first trip was quite an adventure too, as I was in New York traveling alone and doing the sights. I had also been to New Jersey on business, just not Atlantic City, New Jersey.

Fast forward 25 years. I started looking at what was available with Armed Forces Vacation Club. There was a beautiful Wyndham Resort two blocks from the Boardwalk and ocean, so I booked a one bedroom condo.

I booked a flight to Laguardia Airport and a shuttle to the Port Authority in Manhattan where I would then take a bus to Atlantic City, New Jersey. The flight was less expensive flying in to New York than Atlantic City and I would also get a chance to spend a little time in Manhattan. A bonus for me.

I arrived in the morning and a Cardiologist friend of mine picked me up at the airport and we toured Queens. I had never been to Queens on any of my visits to New York. We had lunch at a really cool neighborhood diner and then took off to Manhattan. I found it all to to be very exciting.

When it was time for me to catch my bus, my friend dropped me off at the Port Authority. This was where, three days later, there was a bombing attempt. It was all over the news. Matt called me to make sure I was still in New Jersey and didn't plan on traveling back that day!

The Port Authority is a busy hub and there are hundreds, if not thousands, of people that go through there on a daily basis from all the neighboring cities. The only rude person I encountered was at the Information Desk. Go figure. You would think they would hire someone that was not only friendly but with excellent customer service skills. That was definitely not the case on this cold December day.

Despite the clerks lack of help, through the help of total strangers, I was able to find my bus. This was not like any terminal I had ever been in. It had several levels, many ticket windows for buses to go to other cities, both in New York and all over the United States.

I took an elevator to the ground floor and saw a very long line to a Greyhound bus that was going to Atlantic City. I was struggling with luggage on top of being lost in a huge building full of people bustling to get to their buses. Welcome to New York City!

I finally got on the third bus and settled in for the ride to Atlantic City. The bus driver told me to sit in the front seat. I guess he detected my southern accent and knew I would feel more comfortable up front. I was grateful for his kindness.

After we got out of Manhattan and were clearly on the freeway, the driver was going to give us information about the ride to Atlantic City. He started of by telling us that 55 years ago, to the day, he came into this world. Without skipping a beat, the entire bus erupted with an enthusiastic rendition of "Happy Birthday". I, of course, joined in and it was the coolest thing I had ever witnessed on a bus or any form of public transportation. The driver thanked everyone and then proceeded to tell us how long it would take to get to Atlantic City and what stops he would be making upon arrival. About 15 minutes from Atlantic City, snow began to fall and it was beautiful.

Upon arrival at the Bus Depot it was still snowing lightly and was very cold!

I retrieved my luggage, tipped the driver and then called an Uber. The Uber arrived pretty quickly, but it was on the next block, so I had to struggle with my luggage and "walk" a block to meet my Uber. Grrrr.

The drive to the resort was quick and uneventful. I checked in and took my luggage to my condo and just dropped it off. I was starving. I hadn't eaten since noon and it was almost eleven p.m.

I found out there were not any restaurants in the resort but just a block away was a bar/restaurant that was still open. I walked to the restaurant in the snow. It rarely snows where I live in Little Rock, so this was fun to me.

I wanted to order something light, but wouldn't you know it, the kitchen had closed just before I arrived. I had ordered a beer and so I asked if they had any chips. The bartender went back in the kitchen and came out with a menu and said they would cook something for me. Wow, that was so nice. I guess I looked hungry.

I ordered the simplest thing I could find on the menu. I thought Nachos shouldn't be that much trouble and, at that point, I wasn't going to be picky. Everyone in the bar was friendly and I made a mental note to come back there earlier on another evening. Before the kitchen had closed.

I walked back to the highrise resort, took a shower, and snuggled up in my very comfortable king size bed. It felt wonderful after my long day of travel.

The next morning, I took the time to look over the condo. As usual, it was a beautiful and had all the comforts of home. I then looked online for a shopping center, one with a grocery store or a dollar store and set out to get a few supplies to have in the condo.

A few blocks south and over a block was a dollar general, grocery store and a Little Caesars. I purchased my usual supplies of diet coke, frozen breakfast food, a bag of cookies, and a couple of other snacks to have in the condo.

I saw a couple of cute Christmas t-shirts too, so I bought a couple for gifts. I took all that back to the condo and then decided to take a bus to see what was in the area.

The front desk had given me some Jitney Bus tickets someone had left with them, so I was ready to go. The tickets were for Seniors. 55 and over. The ticket price was 75 cents. Regular price for the bus ride was $1.50 and the buses went to the area Casinos down the main drag and back.

The Jitney Busses were small and held maybe twenty Passengers. They ran about every 15 minutes, so it was an inexpensive way to get around town. I didn't need to rent a car!

I asked the driver where I could purchase more tickets and he referred me to one of the check cashing places that was on the bus route. I stopped at one and purchased a sheet of ten tickets for $7.50.

I decided to get off the bus at one the big Casinos and had lunch in one of their restaurants. I got back on a Jitney Bus and headed back towards my resort.

It was cold, but with a coat on, it was bearable, so I walked the couple of blocks to the Boardwalk. I wanted to see the beach, take some pictures, and look at the souvenir shops. I met one of the Boardwalk Ambassadors, Dwight, and he told me a little about the history of the boardwalk. Then I picked up souvenirs for friends and family. The usual.

I went back to my resort and started looking online for show tickets. I bought a ticket to see The Three Tenors. I was determined to see those Tenors. It was snowing when it was time to leave for the show so I called an Uber. Little did I know it, but the casino I was going to was only a block and a half away. I could have walked.

The tickets and show were great, with one exception. There was a man sitting in front of me that was very distracting. He was singing along, very loudly. People were asking him to be quiet.

He looked back at me and I made a shushing gesture. He then flipped me off! I didn't say a word to him and he acted so rudely to me. I looked around for security but there wasn't anyone to be found.

The man was apparently intoxicated but he didn't act rudely to any of the men telling him to be quiet. I guess he thought they would start a fight. He apparently thought, because I was a woman and a lot smaller than he was, he would take advantage of the situation and be rude to me.

After the show, I found the manager and told him what happened. He said, since it was a Christmas Show, they had cut back on security.

The show tickets were $65 and I explained to the manager that might not be a lot of money for some people but it was for me. He apologized and told me he would comp another show for me and any of my friends to make up for it. He said The Jersey Tenors would be playing Thursday through the weekend.

I told him I was from Arkansas and was traveling alone and had already purchased a ticket for the Jersey Tenors too.

I went back Thursday to see the Jersey Tenors and the Manager had given my name to the Assistant Manager. She asked where I would like to sit. I said I would like to be down front. She escorted me to the front row, center stage.

That show was fantastic! Nobody causing a scene! I loved the show, and went to the lobby after and had my picture made with the group. I definitely left with a better impression after the show.

The next day I went back to the Boardwalk and ran into Dwight, the Boardwalk Ambassador. We had a nice conversation about this being his retirement job and all that it entailed. He asked me if I would have lunch with him. I said I would like that.

We walked to a nearby Casino where they had a food court and we picked out a place to eat. Dwight was a perfect gentleman. We swapped phone numbers before lunch was over and we still stay in touch.

I was walking through another Casino after lunch and a "show girl" in full holiday costume and make-up gave me a discount coupon for a Christmas show that was starting in an hour.

I went to the box office and bought a ticket and went and saw the best Christmas variety show. What a treat that was. The girls and costumes were beautiful, and the music included all the holiday favorites.

After the show, the show girls were in the lobby to take pictures with the guests, so I had my pictures taken with a couple of them. They were all very sweet.

After the show I found the closest stop to catch a Jitney Bus. I just needed to walk to the corner.

It didn't seem to matter what time of day it was, I would miss a bus by minutes. So if you want to catch the bus, just go out to the stop five minutes before me.

I was going to take the Greyhound bus to New York the next day and take a night tour of the city. I went to the corner, not even at the bus stop, and a Jitney Bus stopped where I was standing. I said I was going to cross the street and get a bus going the opposite direction. The driver told me to get in and he would call the driver and meet him and I could change buses. He said, "It's too cold to be standing outside." He wouldn't take my bus ticket. He said, "Save it and give it to the other driver."

He got on his radio and called the other driver and arranged a meeting place. When he got there, he stopped and let me cross the street to get the other bus.

I couldn't believe he went to so much trouble to be so kind to a tourist. That was one of the nicest things anyone had ever done for me. Wow.

I got to the bus station and it was full of homeless people. The police came in and had them clear out. The city apparently let them stay till morning to get out of the cold.

I caught my bus and went to Manhattan. It was only eight a.m. when I got there so I looked around for a place to have breakfast.

I had been to New York in December before, but this was the coldest I had ever been in my life. I was dressed in jeans, boots, sweater, coat, wool scarf, and wool gloves and I was still freezing. I saw a Burger King and crossed the street to get to it. Quickly! There was a sign that said you could only stay there 30 minutes. I guess homeless people took advantage of going in out of the cold there too.

I sat in the seat next to an older gentleman and we struck up a conversation. He was a very nice man and we shared stories, where we lived, etc. He lived in Manhattan.

After my 30 minutes was up, I went in search of a tour. I bought a ticket for a day tour and a night tour. It was a savings if you purchased both. I thought it would at least keep me out of the cold, so I took both day tours.

It was afternoon when I had completed both tours, so I began my search for a place to grab a late lunch. I saw a nice deli on the corner and went in. It was pretty crowded but the self serve line was short. I picked out a 6 inch ham and cheese sub and a diet coke. That was $17 and you didn't get any chips with it either. Welcome to New York!

After my late lunch, I was going to walk around and maybe go to Rockefeller Center. It was so cold, brrrrr. I decided to skip Rockefeller Center and the night tour and go back to Atlantic City. I had seen Rockefeller Center on previous trips at Christmas time.

Usually my trips are from Saturday to Saturday. This one was from Monday to Monday, so I went to a beautiful Catholic church a couple of blocks from the resort for Mass on Sunday.

After Mass I went to a nice neighborhood diner on the way back to my resort and had a wonderful breakfast.

Later, that evening, I tried to find another church in the neighborhood that had an advertised Christmas Show. Here I am walking the streets of Atlantic City at night in search of the church. I finally gave up, but got lots of exercise.

On Monday, I called an Uber, went back to the bus depot, took the trip to the port authority in Manhattan, and got a shuttle to LaGuardia. The traffic in Manhattan was at a standstill. It was a 45 minute ride instead of a 15 minute ride. I was really getting nervous about making it in time for my flight.

I got to the airport with only minutes to spare. But I made the flight. Whew! That last day in Manhattan made me realize that it was a fun city to visit, but I wouldn't want to live there.

CHAPTER FOURTEEN
Toronto – Niagara Falls

Are you looking for Chapter 13? Stop looking. In keeping with superstitions about the number 13, I am not including it. In some countries, as it is here in the United States, the number 13 is considered unlucky and building owners will sometimes purposely omit a floor numbered 13. Hence, the 13th floor is sometimes given the number 14.

Where do I want to go next? I've never been to Niagara Falls or Toronto, Canada. I started looking at AFVC. They had resorts in Canada, but not one in the Niagara Falls area so I looked at Toronto and struck out there too.

I went on Hotels.com and found the cutest "guest house" and decided to book it. It was in a great area of the city, or I thought it was anyway. I went online and got a ridiculously low fare on Justfly.com for $280 roundtrip from Little Rock.

Next on my list was "Things to do in Toronto". I looked at tours to Niagara Falls and found a reasonably priced day tour with pick up at my guest house to Niagara Falls. I booked it. I found my usual double decker tour bus and booked a two day tour. You can usually get a discount from the day rate to a two day rate.

I then looked at the other area attractions. I booked a tall ship Harbor Cruise. I wanted to visit the CN Tower and go to a Blue Jay baseball game. I decided I would book other sights and things to do when I got to Toronto.

On the double decker tour I knew I would see the CN Tower. The next item was a Blue Jay baseball game. The stadium is located next to the CN Tower and is called the Rogers Centre. I went online to Groupon and purchased a ticket to a game at half price.

Between the tours, tall ship cruise, the baseball game, dining out, and shopping, I thought that was enough to fill my week.

Again, so excited about my trip. I booked my ticket online for the train from the airport and purchased subway tickets on site. Taxi fare from the airport would range from $60 - $75. Remember, I am traveling on a retirement budget. I also figured it would be more fun to take the train and subway.

I arrived at approximately 11:00 p.m. and there was an entrance to the train at the airport. That was easy. When I got to the city, the subway station was where the train stopped. So far, so good.

When I got to my subway stop, I unloaded my luggage and found the exit to the street. Upstairs! Luckily there was an escalator and I was pulling my luggage with wheels (Thank you Matt).

As soon as I got to the street level, I started looking around and asked a young man on the street, instead of asking a homeless person, which direction Gloucester street was.

He gave me directions and said he was going that way and would walk with me. He offered to help me with my bags. I told him I could manage but thanked him.

So we were walking down the street at close to midnight, me pulling my luggage. Surprisingly enough, there were quite a few people walking and quite a few bars and restaurants were still open.

When we got to within two blocks of Gloucester, the young man pointed to where it was and we parted ways. Nice first impression of Canada. I passed several couples, guys actually, it was predominantly known as a gay community. I felt very safe.

I finally got to the Victoria Mansion Guest House. It was a beautiful Victorian style house with 22 rooms with private baths. I had been given a code for the door as the desk would not be open past 7:00 p.m. In the foyer was a row of mailboxes. I had a code to get in the box and retrieved the front door key and my room key.

I was relieved that my room was on the ground floor because there wasn't an elevator. Little did I know, the ground floor was two small staircases down. Ugh. I had to make two trips to get my luggage downstairs. Finally I was in my room!

It was "cute". I had a single bed, bedside table, desk, phone, chifferobe, bathroom, microwave, a few dishes, and a coffee maker. All the comforts of home without the five star price. I was exhausted from my trip, so I went to bed. As some older folks might say, I must have died because I slept like a baby.

I woke up at about 8:00 a.m. Fairly late for me. I showered and dressed and took off on foot to find breakfast.

I found the coolest restaurant that was full of twenty/thirty year olds. There was a wait, so I asked if I could sit at the bar. They had eggs benedict on the menu, so I knew what I was having for breakfast. I drank a diet coke instead of one of their favorites, Bloody Mary's or a Mimosa. I am not a big drinker and didn't want to start my day with a "buzz".

After breakfast I decided to find my tour bus. This area at one end was full of old style Victorian houses, apartment buildings, and then, before you knew it, you were in an area that looked like downtown, with high rise buildings, restaurants, coffee shops, and hotels.

I found the bus stop for the tour buses. My first day was filled with lots of trivia and information about Toronto and Canada in general. I was surprised to find Toronto looked a lot like Manhattan and was told that it was a location for many films, actually more than Hollywood. They said Toronto was used quite often when a location was supposed to be Manhattan.

One of the differences was they had to bring in "yellow cabs". A way to tell the difference for sure was if the director missed a street car in the background. Manhattan doesn't have streetcars.

Hollywood executives say they go to Canada because of a favorable exchange rate and generous subsidies, but choose University of Toronto because of their wide variety of buildings and its resemblance to Ivy League schools.

Ron Howard recreated a 1930's Central Park for his movie "Cinderella Man" amid the rolling meadows of the University of Toronto Scarborough campus. You should google "Why Hollywood loves U of T".

It has an interesting article with too much information to share in my book.

One interesting tidbit I learned on my tour was that the name Toronto is pronounced by the locals with a soft t or no t sound at the end of the word. They say they can tell a visitor by the way they pronounce Toronto with a strong "tow" sound at the end of the word.

I took my tall ship cruise, just barely making it in time. I actually "ran" to get there before the ship was scheduled to leave. It was a beautiful cruise, although a little cool and windy. I had always wanted to go on a tall ship (sailing vessel). The "Kajama" looked like something out of the movie "Pirates of the Caribbean". The Kajama was a traditional 165 foot three masted schooner.

After we left the harbor, passengers were recruited to help hoist the sails. We sailed on the Toronto Harbor as well as beautiful Lake Ontario. The skyline of Toronto was always in sight.

It was late afternoon and, although the sun was still out, there was a breeze and I wished I had brought a hoodie or a jacket. It was a little chilly for me.

The water was smooth, and none of the passengers were belted in or wore life jackets. All of the passengers sat on bench-like seats alongside the rail or in the center of the ship on what appeared to be large wood boxes next to the huge masts.

Even though we didn't wear life jackets, I just assumed the life jackets were stored in the wood boxes.

There was a full bar as well as a snack bar on board. Other than that, you had the look and feel of a real pirate ship.

I took lots of selfies and pictures of the Toronto skyline. I am a bit of a fanatic when it comes to pictures. I have thousands of them saved to my phone. Over 6,000 really!

I stopped in at the "Amsterdam Brew House" after my cruise to have dinner before returning to the guest house. The place was packed so I did what I often do. I sat at the bar. As a rule you can sit at the bar and dine and you don't have a wait. I had a delicious hamburger! It was huge and I was stuffed.

My Niagara Falls tour was scheduled for the next day. They had a car to pick me up and take me to the tour office. We got on a beautiful

Limo Bus from there. The bus seated about 30. I sat right behind the driver. Most people were in groups of two or four. I was alone.

The driver showed a young man to a seat next to me as he was alone too. We struck up a conversation and I learned he was from Brazil, was married, and his name was Eduardo.

We ended up taking the Hornblower cruise together, along with probably 200 other passengers. The boat was full, and we were all issued plastic ponchos. We were to be going so close to the falls you would get soaked without the ponchos.

We took pictures of each other and a couple together. Eduardo was young enough to be my son, so don't get any crazy ideas. We had a nice time sharing stories and pictures.

People seem to be amazed that I travel alone most of the time. The thing of it is, I usually meet the nicest and most interesting people when I am alone. So I am not alone for long.

The Hornblower cruise was so much fun. The water was like an ice cold shower. Before we left we were told what to expect because, when we were on the boat, especially right at the falls, it was so loud with the sound of the rushing water.

We were on a large two deck tug boat. It was loud, as were the excited 200 passengers. We went within just a few feet of the falls. Even with the ponchos, we still felt the icy cold water and the spray was like being under a shower. We all got wet, if not soaked.

We kept our phones and cameras under the ponchos when we were right by the falls. It was amazing to be so close to such gorgeous and powerful waterfalls. After the hornblower cruise, we took pictures from all angles, trying to capture the beauty of it all. We found a hot dog stand and got a hot dog with all the fixin's and a soft drink and ate at an outdoor area with short brick walls around flower beds.

When I was growing up, you heard of people going to Niagara Falls on their honeymoon. I waited till I was 70 years old and went alone.

The next day I went to the CN Tower. It is still one of the largest freestanding towers in the Northern Hemisphere. Over 1800 ft high. Its location is a couple of blocks from the wharf and easy to find from the subway or rail cars.

I think I mentioned I was afraid of heights. In fact, a psychologist told me it was really the fear of falling. That made sense. I love to fly, had been to the top of the Empire State Building, Top of the St Louis Arch, the Eiffel Tower, Grand Canyon, been on the 550 foot "High Roller" Ferris Wheel in Las Vegas, the London Eye, the Orlando Eye, and got married in a hot air balloon. So this should be a piece cake.

It was a fun experience and we got to view and take pictures of the beautiful city of Toronto as well as the Toronto Harbour. The Tower had an area with a "glass floor" at the top of the tower. I had someone snap a picture of me standing on it. Quickly. It was a little scary. I was hoping there weren't any flaws in the construction of it. I was actually gritting my teeth in my picture, although it looked like a toothy smile.

The next day I went to find a "Blue Jay" shirt to wear to the game. I was in a store called "Winners". It was a department store downtown across from the Eaton Center, a beautiful three story mall that covered probably two blocks. I found a ladies T-shirt for $12. Yay!

I went back to my room and discovered on the way that my phone was missing. Oh no. I lost another phone, with all my contacts and my pictures from my Toronto trip.

These pictures had not been saved to the Cloud and I was just sick. After shedding a few tears, I called the store. Nothing had been turned in.

I had purchased a pair of slacks and they left the security tag on them, so the next morning I headed back to Winners. When I went in the store, the alarm went off but the manager was at the door and knew I was coming in, not walking out with stolen merchandise. When I explained that the security tag was left on my purchased item, I then explained that I was in the day before and knew I left my phone at the number one cashier station. She said she would look.

She looked in all the places it "should" have been and a couple of places it "shouldn't" have been and all of a sudden she lifted my phone out of a drawer full of junk. OMG! My Phone! I started crying and thanking her. I got my phone and all my pictures back! I was so happy and thankful. Saying a prayer of thanks!

I went downstairs and asked a security guard where I could find a payphone. I had been surprised to see payphones in the city when on my tour. One was right across the street.

I crossed the street and called AT&T and asked them to reactivate my phone. I had reported it lost the day before. Within minutes, my phone was restored! I was thrilled beyond words. My contacts, my pictures, everything! I guarded my phone with my life from that point on.

I decided to have lunch downtown. I went to a Caribbean jerk chicken restaurant and had the best, most tender jerk chicken. Like they say in the South, "It made you want to slap your mama".

When touring Toronto I saw a playhouse featuring the play "Potted Potter: an Unauthorized Harry Experience", a parody by Dan and Jeff, so I called and purchased a ticket.

I purchased one of the least expensive tickets available and it was on the 2nd Balcony or the third floor. The ticket agent cautioned me about the height. I said it wouldn't be a problem and bought the ticket.

I went back to my room and got ready to go see "Potted Potter."

When I went in the theater I realized why she cautioned me... in case I had vertigo. The balcony was a metal ramp with one row of seats and was attached or bolted to the wall three stories up. Whoa! There goes my fear of heights.

We were literally hanging on the wall. I was okay, but it took a few minutes to get accustomed to being up so high. It might have helped that I had gone next door to the theater before the show and had a drink.

I am always early, and holding true to form, I had an hour to kill. Next door was a bar, pool room, upstairs patio. I went in and nobody was there. I didn't know at first there was a rooftop patio and that's where all the customers were.

It was a beautiful evening, not dark yet, so I stuck my head out the patio door to see if there were any seats available. Much to my surprise, there were were four men ranging in ages from twenties to sixties waving to me and summoning me to join them. I did.

After the introductions I said I was waiting to go to the play next door. They were all perfect gentlemen and we laughed and shared stories. I had to leave to make the play but it was another fun experience.

Potted Potter was apparently hilarious to many of the young patrons. I found it to be a little insulting. I am a huge Harry Potter fan and didn't enjoy all the humor. Oh well, it was another experience in Canada.

The theater was just a few blocks from the Guest House, so I walked back to my room.

I wanted a Diet Coke and something sweet, so I crossed the busy street from my home away from home. I bought a Diet Coke and a candy bar. The candy bar was $1.75 and the diet coke was about $3.50. Wow. No dollar store around there.

A sad thing occurred on my bus tour. We were on a busy street and a few cars from the corner a female cyclist had been hit by a truck, minutes before our arrival. No emergency personnel had arrived yet. It was clear that it was a fatality. I lowered my head and started to pray for that young woman's family.

I had never witnessed anything like that and was so upset. After the tour ended, I went back to the guest house, in no mood to go anywhere. A little later, I went to the store to get a sandwich and stayed in for the evening. The story was on the news. The young woman was only thirty years old and a truck ran a red light and ran into her. A sad night.

The next day was the Blue Jays game. I put on my Blue Jay t-shirt and shorts and took the subway to the arena. It was called Rogers Center, a beautiful arena that was on the adjoining property to the CN Tower. The atmosphere was like going to the fair. Lines forming at every entrance, vendors outside selling hot dogs, drinks, banners, hats, shirts, etc.

I had been to the CN Tower on another visit, but sat on a bench looking up at the tower while waiting for time to go in the arena. Two sweet older ladies approached the bench. There was only room for one so I offered my seat to the them.

We, of course, struck up a conversation. I learned that they were from England and were on a 6 week trip to the United States and Canada. Both were retired. I took their pictures and then we took some selfies together. We had the best time getting to know each other and exchanged email addresses and I emailed the pictures to them.

It was time to go in the arena for the game. The arena was a dome like structure. The weather was beautiful so the dome was open. I heard a funny story about the new arena on the tour bus.

The tour guide said when the first game was held at the arena, the dome was initially closed. The crowd starting chanting "Open the Dome", "Open the Dome". So, the operator opened the Dome.

It takes 30 minutes to open the dome completely and 30 minutes to close it, after it had completely opened.

Apparently there wasn't any concern or knowledge that it was raining outside. The Dome started opening and the rain came in. It took 30 minutes to finish opening and another 30 minutes to close it again. The crowd got soaked!

The night I was there, the skies were clear and it was a beautiful night for a ball game. The game was between "The Washington Nationals" and the Toronto Blue Jays.

Before the game started they played "our" National anthem. The Star Spangled Banner. I was so impressed with the crowd. They all stood, took off their caps and those that knew the words, sang. They showed such respect. Then they played the Canadian National Anthem. The same respect was shown, caps off, everybody singing. It was beautiful beginning to a great game. I was so proud to be a part of the crowd. It turned out to be an exciting game.

At one point half way into the game, the entire stadium stood and enthusiastically sang "Take me out to the Ballgame"! That was another cool moment of my trip.

The day I was to leave Canada I had to be at the subway at 4:30 a.m. It was Sunday and it hadn't occurred to me that the subway didn't run that early. There I was with my luggage at a locked door to the subway. I saw a bus and hurried to the corner and got on the bus. I explained to the driver that I was trying to get to Union Station to catch a train to get to the airport. Still not willing to pay $60 -$75. She said "let me see if Union Station is open this early". She told the passengers that she was going to stop the bus to use the phone. She found out that Union Station was open and started the bus again. I got off at the corner from Union Station and was unsuccessful in finding an unlocked door. I of course was struggling with my luggage, up and down stairs and out of breath when I saw someone going in a door about a third of a block down the street. I hurried to that door, went in and was greeted by a security guard. He noticed I was out of breath and asked if he could help. I told him I needed a train to the airport. He directed me to a ticket counter and there was a train "sitting" with the doors open. The train was to leave in 10 minutes. Praise God. I stored my luggage and sat back being thankful again. Thank you Lord.

I made it in plenty of time to catch my flight. We went through customs in Canada instead of in the United States. That was unusual I thought. I hadn't had anything to eat so I looked around for a snack stand or restaurant. I was directed down a hall. I saw it was down a hall, then an elevator and down another long hall before giving up and going back upstairs. There was a newstand with candy and nuts and soft drinks. So breakfast was a candy bar and diet coke. A "breakfast of champions". This would have to tide me over till I got to Chicago. At the Chicago airport I had to walk miles, of course, or so it seemed, to get to my gate, so I stopped and grabbed a breakfast sandwich on the run. I made my connection and was on my way to Little Rock. Relief, again. Home sweet home!

CHAPTER FIFTEEN

Las Vegas — Red Rock Canyon — Online Dating

Okay, so how does all this relate? Well I met the nicest person on a dating site and he lived in Las Vegas. We talked on the phone and texted each other and just had fun visiting. He asked me to come to Las Vegas to see him. I booked a hotel room on Hotwire, a flight on Southwest, and my rental car on Hotwire; I was all set to go to Las Vegas.

His name is Richard. We are the same age and related to so many of the same things. Humor, music, expressions, etc. He was so much fun. I knew we would have a good time in Vegas.

Richard met me at the airport, even though I told him I had a rental car. He drove to my hotel and I followed him. He lived in Las Vegas and knew exactly where my hotel was.

We dropped off my car and headed to Freemont Street. I had booked a zipline and had an appointment time at 8:00 p.m. I went in the office and picked up my ticket. Richard didn't want to zipline, so he stayed below and watched me.

I did the laydown zipline, or Zoomline, which was the highest line. It was 114 feet in the air and traveled 1700 feet, Superhero style. I think I mentioned what a chicken I am, but I was determined to do this.

Three people go at a time, so I was teamed up with the sweetest couple from Boston. The young lady was tiny. I told her she might get stuck because she was so little. She said, "but I weigh 95 pounds!" I told her, "Sweetheart, my right leg weighs 95 pounds!" She got stopped about twenty five feet from the end and one of the employees had to go out on a line and pull her in. I didn't mean to jinx her.

I hadn't paid too much attention to the riders that didn't have to be pulled in, so when it came to an abrupt halt at the end, I thought something was wrong. It comes to a jerking halt, you hang there for a couple of minutes and then you slowly go in to the end of the ride. It was so much fun, flying over the crowd, under the light show.

After the ride, Richard and I walked along Freemont Street and listened to the various bands in concert. We stopped at one of the sidewalk bars to have a drink and "people watch".

After the Freemont experience, we went to the strip and rode the High Roller, the 550 ft high ferris wheel.

The ride takes 30 minutes for the wheel to rotate once. It cost $24.95 (daytime) and $34.95 (nighttime). It consists of 28 cabins with each holding up to 40 persons. Richard and I were put in a cabin by ourselves. Neither of us were crazy about going up 550 feet but we did it.

We didn't get back to my hotel till 2:00 a.m. and I hadn't checked in yet. I waited in a short line and when it was my turn, they couldn't find my room or reservation. The clerk apologized and said they were going to have to let me stay in one of their timeshares. I didn't know what that meant really, but accepted the key and headed to the elevator. Richard helped me with my bags and left me at the elevator. A perfect gentleman.

I got off the elevator and found my door. When I walked in, I was pleasantly surprised. Instead of a hotel room, I had the most beautiful condo I had ever seen. Crystal chandeliers, leather furniture, stainless steel appliances, king size bed, two flat screen TV's, a four by four jacuzzi tub, huge bathroom, a gazillion towels, shower with mirror for shaving, safe, and a washer/dryer. The mirror across from the jacuzzi was framed with a 4 ft wide 8 ft high silver frame. There was an Elvis print in the dining room and also a print of Marilyn Monroe. It was too perfect!

The next morning, the maid knocked on my door. I told her that I would be leaving in about thirty minutes but I didn't need maid service because I didn't even get to the room till about 2:30 a.m. and I was alone. She asked if I needed any fresh towels. Can you imagine? There were probably twenty towels in the bathroom. Bath towels, hand towels, and washcloths. I couldn't have possibly used all those towels unless I had a family of four with me.

After the conversation with the maid, I got dressed, went downstairs to a lovely formal dining room, and ordered eggs benedict. I splurged. My breakfast was $32 before the tip.

This hotel was the WestGate and was formerly the International years ago. Elvis performed there for many years. The first time I saw Elvis in concert was at the International in 1969.

There was a lifesize bronze statue of Elvis in the lobby and life sized pictures in the lobby and all the hallways. I was in hog heaven. As an Elvis fan, I was one happy female! I got my first kiss and scarf from Elvis in 1973 in Monroe, Louisiana. I was the only one in the arena to get kissed or get a scarf. I had no idea I would be surrounded with Elvis memorabilia in my hotel.

Richard and I talked and he picked me up at the hotel and we went to Red Rock Canyon. I had never seen anything so beautiful since moving to Arkansas. We drove the 12.5 mile scenic route and stopped and took pictures along the way. It was a wonderful afternoon.

On the way back to Las Vegas, we took the road that passed the Bonnie Springs Ranch. This was a small western town that offered Wild West shows, trail rides, and picturesque backdrops. We stopped and took pictures in front of the old stagecoach.

We stopped at a Mexican Restaurant for dinner and, when we got back to my hotel, I invited Richard up to see my condo and to give him the hospitality gifts I had brought him from Arkansas. We had a glass of wine and said goodnight. Another nice day.

The next morning, maybe closer to noon, Richard picked me up and we went out for breakfast. Richard wanted to show me a restaurant called Blueberry Hill. There are several locations in Las Vegas. My favorite location is at 1280 S. Decatur Blvd.

My son, his wife, and my girlfriend went there with me on another Las Vegas visit. My favorite waitress is Susie. She is from New Jersey and is not only efficient, but very entertaining.

On this particular visit I had placed my order, but decided I wanted something more. I asked if I could add something to my order. Susie said "No. You've already ordered." I cracked up. Of course she let me add the pancake I wanted. She brought it out very quickly. When she saw I wasn't eating it, she asked why and I said I actually wanted it after my egg dish. So, Susie promptly picked up the dish and gave it to my son and daughter-in-law. They shared it. They said it was delicious.

Susie brought my pancake "after" I had eaten my egg dish. It was also delicious.

Everytime I go to Las Vegas, I go to that restaurant and see Susie. You can get the best breakfast in town and all the staff is friendly. Even Susie.

Every time I go to town, if Richard is in town, we have lunch or dinner and go to Red Rock Canyon.

I told Richard I was going to mention him in my book. He said "if its a nice comment, put my first and last name and phone number. I could use the advertisement. If it's not nice, just use my first name."

CHAPTER SIXTEEN
Handy Hints and Packing, I'm No Expert!

Trust me; you will find a lot better sources for packing outside of this chapter, but they work for me.

Packing for a cruise is a lot different than packing for other trips. The consideration for paying for luggage on flights is a definite consideration, as well as the length of your trip.

I believe I've mentioned that I've been on 34 cruises and I'm not one of those people that take one large bag. How do they do that? I have cut back considerably over the years, but I still over pack and always come home with things I never wore.

I try to limit my colors. I wear black a lot. My favorite color. Is black a color or a lack of color? Or the presence of all colors? When you select black evening wear, you can also limit your shoes and purses to black. I am a bit of a clothes freak, so I won't ever wear a garment more than once, even if its laundered on the trip.

One very nice perk I have with Carnival Cruise Line is free laundry and folding service. I was a Platinum level passenger for years. You get to that level by traveling 75 days at sea. As a Platinum guest you were allowed two bags of laundry done free.

A couple of years ago it was three bags. You would be surprised at how much clothing you can put in a laundry bag if you roll it up and pack it very tightly. I can turn in two bags and get three bags back any day of the week.

I recently acquired the level of Diamond on Carnival. As a Diamond guest you have "unlimited" laundry done free. Yay Diamond! To be a Diamond guest, you have to have sailed for 200 days. I never thought I would get there, but on my January Hawaii cruise, I made it.

In the not-too-many-years-ago past, the airport personnel would spot check bags and you might have to open your luggage and they would rifle through it. Looking for what? Drugs? Weapons? Who knows anymore. I didn't want the airport personnel touching my under things, so I started packing my underwear in gallon size zip close baggies.

I realized how nicely it kept things so I enlarged my list to shoes, evening bags, toiletries, etc. It kept my luggage so neat, so I still do that.

When carrying a hanging clothing bag for my dresses, jumpsuits, and blouses, I put 3 and sometimes 4 or 5 items on the same hanger and usually put a plastic cleaner bag over those items. When I get on the ship I would transfer some of them to the ship hangers. Hanging them that way helps to keep them from getting wrinkled and lightens the weight in the clothing bag. 50 lb limit to each bag.

I sometimes put shoes or boots in the bottom of this bag and toiletries in the side pockets. If you put your toiletries in baggies, you prevent your clothes from getting wet if something leaks.

As I pack each piece of luggage, I have a sheet of paper on top of the open bag and list what I packed. I usually pack a few days early before a trip and if I have a list, I don't have to go through the bag, messing up my items to see what I previously packed.

Unpacking is much easier as well as repacking at the end of your trip. I am not going to live out of a suitcase for seven days and my trips are at least seven days. I want to live like I am at home. Baggies keep things neat in drawers as well as keeps them clean, if you are concerned with your drawers not being pristine. My cabin mate for my Hawaii cruise was OCD and refused to use a drawer for fear of getting "cooties". Sorry Melissa. I had to tell that. So she lived out of a suitcase and I had all the drawer space. Cool. Worked for me.

I always take extra plastic bags (Thank you Walmart) for dirty clothes. They are transferred to ship laundry bags when sending laundry out. I put shoes in Walmart bags too when they won't fit in a gallon size baggie.

I have the coolest travel jewelry bags that I bought on a cruise. They are approximately 4"x4"x4". They have eight zippered pockets that fold over each other and the entire bag zips shut. They are in different colors. I have two that are in animal print and one is black. They are so convenient and you can carry tons of jewelry and decide exactly what you want to wear on the trip instead of before the trip.

The downfall with handy little jewelry cases? I was going to Puerto Vallarta and the airline said there was limited space in the overhead and they would check our carry on luggage at no charge and we could pick it up at our final destination. So I took advantage of this and thought "Good, I don't have to struggle with bags at my connection."

I got to Puerto Vallarta and my carry-on didn't make it. The airline said they would deliver it to my resort. Well, it showed up at 10 p.m. I arrived at 1:00 p.m.

When I opened my bag, I immediately saw it had been tampered with and all my jewelry was missing. I was sick. The majority of it was costume jewelry, but if you've checked prices lately, that can add up to a lot of money if you have a lot of it. I only lost two diamond pieces. More sentimental value than money value, but I was sick over it being lost or stolen.

I called the airline and reported the loss and sent documentation to the airline when I was home again. It took three months to get reimbursed. Luckily I had "selfies" with every piece of jewelry and was able to document what it was, where it was purchased, and for what amount. I sent pictures. It was a little over a thousand dollars.

They actually wanted receipts. Who keeps a receipt for years? My fine jewelry was a gift and I had it for years and probably didn't have a receipt in the first place.

I still check my carry on when available. Oh well, I'll take my chances.

If you are doing as much traveling as I've been doing, you might want to make sure you get the post office to hold your mail. I happen to have a sweet son and daughter-in-law that live within two miles of me and they drop by and either pick up my mail and hold it or put it on my kitchen table.

I always text my friends/neighbors across the street and tell them when I will be out of town or country. I tell them if they see a U-Haul out front, I'm not moving and they should call the police.

Another savings if you have a family close by is transportation to and from the airport. With very few exceptions, my sons have taken me to the airport and I don't have to pay parking for a week. Parking at the airport for 17 days on my trips to Europe would have been really expensive.

If I go very early in the morning, I will take an Uber or drive and park and they will pick my car up later so I only have to pay parking for just a few hours.

When I book my trips I type up an itinerary and email it to my sons and girlfriends. One time I had a text from one of my sons asking if I had power at my house during a storm. I responded "I don't know, I'm in Reno, haven't you looked at my itinerary?"

Last, but not least, when you are in another country and have small bills or coins left over, don't worry about exchanging them, they make good souvenirs for your grandkids.

CHAPTER SEVENTEEN

Las Vegas – Grand Canyon

I was ready for another trip to Las Vegas. It was February 2018. I booked my condo at the Wyndham Grand Desert just down the street from the Hard Rock Hotel.

It was a nice 1 bedroom condo, not as large as some resorts I've stayed in, but had everything I needed. This condo had a kitchen/living room combination, separate bedroom and bath and had a washer and dryer at a cost of $349 for 7 days with AFVC.

I rented a car on Hotwire.com. A really nice SUV with less than 2,000 miles on it.

I got in touch with my Las Vegas friends and set up dates to visit and have a meal together. I have several favorite restaurants and wanted to go there as well.

One thing I haven't mentioned is my love for ballroom dancing. I usually go to a class or two while in Las Vegas. They have a huge dance community and it is a great place to meet people and have a nice evening.

The first class I attended I met Mark. Mark is an excellent dancer and a great lead. He takes several classes/private lessons during the week.

After class, he said "I'm hungry. I am going out for Mexican food. You want to go?" I replied, "You had me at Mexican". We went to Lindo Michoacan on Flamingo Road. They have wonderful food and the coldest beer in town. I always eat at the bar. Their bartenders are not only friendly and beautiful but have the best service. I make it a point to go there every time I visit Las Vegas. Yum!

I booked a trip to Grand Canyon on Groupon. That trip was at half price. $99 for a full day. The tour bus picked me up at 7:00 a.m. at my resort and we went to the central location of the tour company and were put in groups and loaded on another bus.

The bus wasn't full so I had two seats to myself. Several others were in the same situation. Our driver/tour guide began to tell us what to expect for the day. He explained we would be dropped off at approximately 10 p.m. that night, in the order we were picked up. Guess who was the last person to be picked up? You got it, me.

When we got to the tour office, coffee, juice and snacks were available as well as a ticket line and souvenirs to purchase. I bought my friend (Tim) a couple of T-Shirts that said Route 66 and Grand Canyon. Within thirty minutes we were on our way.

We were headed out towards the Hoover Dam and on to the Grand Canyon. We stopped at a Hardy's for breakfast, got our food to go and got back on the bus. We traveled on Route 66 and went through an historic town with Route 66 signs along the way.

We were looking forward to the approximate 4 hour ride to the Grand Canyon. We stopped at a small town on the way and had lunch. It was a buffet so we were served quickly and after taking a few pictures we were on our way again.

At the stop we had an opportunity to meet and get to know our travel companions on the bus. A young man, was sitting in front of me and asked if I would like to move up and sit with him. We introduced ourselves.

His name was Rudolpho and was visiting the U.S. from Brazil. Rudolpho was single and traveling alone too, so we decided to tour the Grand Canyon together.

This makes it easier for taking pictures of each other and just having someone to enjoy the trip with. Rudolpho was very nice, friendly and a good-looking guy.

Our first stop at the Grand Canyon was on the South Rim. It was one of those moments I felt I needed to "pinch myself". I was really at the Grand Canyon.

We walked down to a look out point and just stood amazed at the beauty all around us. How do you describe something so breathtaking? Something that everyone has seen in pictures and movies all their lives? I wasn't really prepared to be blown away like I was.

Over the years I had many opportunities to go to the Grand Canyon, but because of my fear of heights, I didn't go. It was a thrilling experience. We took tons of pictures with us in them and just scenic pictures with nobody in them.

It is just one of those moments that just taking one picture is definitely not good enough, and for a picture freak like me, several pictures might not be. How many is too many pictures?

Rudolpho had a great camera as well as an Iphone and he took some incredible pictures of us and many scenic views that he shared with me later.

We took selfies together as well as alone. We went to a few different lookout spots. What an incredible view!

Although not fond of heights, I felt very secure at all the lookouts. No chance of falling unless you climb out to somewhere you shouldn't be in the first place.

We heard a story of a man and his family doing just that and the man fell to his death with his family watching. How tragic.

I am not a dare devil so there was no chance of me falling into the Canyon.

We were at the Grand Canyon for at least three hours. We finished up our visit at a lovely gift shop and purchased magnets and postcards as well as getting some more nice pictures of the canyon from inside the shop.

Actually our last stop was in a restaurant/bar where we had a cold drink before getting back on the bus.

After a brief stop at Hardy's for a quick dinner, we settled in for the ride back to Las Vegas.

Just before getting to Hoover Dam, our driver told us to get our cameras ready. We were going to be on the bridge above the dam, not the dam itself.

It was lit up as well as the Dam and was so beautiful at night. I'm not sure my camera caught the image we saw from the bus window.

A nice ending to a nice tour and day at the Grand Canyon. Rudolpho and I exchanged phone numbers and shared pictures of our day.

The next day I went to breakfast at Blueberry Hill and saw Susie. I had a great breakfast before heading out to Planet Hollywood and the Miracle Mile Shops. I looked around at the shops, went into a shop that was only Magnets and made a few purchases.

I had purchased a show ticket to a "Hitzville The Show" for a matinee and a later show of "Marc Savard Comedy Hypnosis".

Hitzville was a musical tribute to favorite Motown artists such as the Jackson 5, Diana Ross and the Supremes, Stevie Wonder, The Marvelettes, Temptations and more. It was a great show. I had an opportunity to get autographs and take pictures with the entertainers after the show.

The Comedy Hypnosis show was one of the best I have seen. Volunteers were on stage and you would not believe some of the things they were made to do. It was hilarious.

The next day my friend Richard took me to brunch at the Paris, across from the Bellagio Fountain Show. Then we went for a drive to Lake Las Vegas and from there we went to Red Rock Canyon. I think I told you in an earlier chapter that I go to Red Rock Canyon every time I go to Las Vegas.

I met with my friend Jane the next day and we went to the Valley of Fire State park. On the way back I got a text from my friend in Illinois. He was asking for my help. I thought he was in Illinois so I couldn't imagine what I could do.

As it turned out, he was in Las Vegas. He knew I was in Las Vegas but I didn't know he was there so I was shocked, to say the least.

He was in town with his current girlfriend and they had a disagreement that started when she had too much to drink.

He asked me to pick him up in front of the Hard Rock Hotel. He was standing outside in his "sock feet" and no jacket.

He left the hotel in a hurry as she was threatening to call the police. So first thing on the agenda was to get him a pair of shoes.

I had done a bit of shopping on previous visits so I knew where to find a "Ross" store. They are open till 9 p.m. so we were in luck.

We went there and I bought him a pair of tennis shoes. I then took him back to the Hard Rock so he could retrieve his luggage.

We then went to my condo to wait for his flight time, at 11:30 p.m. that night. I took him to the airport. He was thankful for my help.

My trips are never dull, but this was crazy. I had planned to have dinner with my friend Jane my last night in town. I've never been one to ignore a call for help from a friend in need, so my plans were changed.

Never a dull moment. I had a restful night after the smoke cleared, and my flight home was scheduled around noon the next day.

CHAPTER EIGHTEEN

Freeport Isn't Across the Bridge from Nassau?

Freeport sounded like a fun place to go for my next trip. I went online at the AFVC website and searched for a resort. I found one called the Island Sea Resort that was right on the beach.

They had a two bedroom 2 bath condo available for $349, so I booked it. I thought it would be fun to get someone to go with me, so I asked my good friend and former co-worker Rebecca. I told her about the condo and asked if she would want to go. She did!

I went online and booked our flights. Only thing, I was apparently confused about where we were going. I was thinking it was Paradise Island, not Freeport.

Paradise Island is across the bridge from Nassau and I had gone there on many cruises. Freeport was approximately 90 miles from Nassau. Uh oh. I had to fix this.

The resort was non-refundable and we needed to get to Freeport from Nassau. So I started checking for transportation. No ferries, but there was a flight available. So I booked a round trip flight from Nassau to Freeport.

It wasn't a bad price. Thank God. I scheduled the return from Nassau to the U.S. a week later in the afternoon, thinking that would give us a day to tour Nassau since Rebecca had not been there.

Rebecca had to get a passport. Luckily we had enough time to accomplish this. I was keeping my grandson Dylan that day so we picked up Rebecca at her office and drove to the post office to get a passport. The passport office was closed. They referred us to the library across the street.

Rebecca talked to the lady that did passports and found out she needed a certified copy of her birth certificate. So off to DHS we go. We waited in an office full of people and our number was like 35. Rebecca was on her lunch hour so it was a bit frustrating. (Dylan was an angel through all of this.)

Rebecca's number finally got called and it was about fifteen more minutes before her birth certificate was ready. We were ready to go back to the library.

The lady at the library took her picture because the one Rebecca had made wasn't the right size she said.

It was time to pay. We had about a month and normally that would be enough time. I got mine in two weeks.

A lot was riding on this passport so I paid to have it expedited. When I first booked the flight I found out that you didn't need a passport to go to Freeport. But...guess what? You needed one to come back into the U.S.

So that's why we were shuffling at the last minute to get the passport. Rebecca paid for the passport and I paid to have it expedited. It's a good thing we did that too. Her passport didn't arrive till the latter part of the week that we were scheduled to fly out.

Rebecca's Dad gave us a ride to the airport. We were on the way!

On our approach to Nassau Rebecca looked out the window and saw the Island and started tearing up. She was excited about our trip and tends to get emotional when we are about to arrive at our destination. Bless her heart.

We checked into customs and then proceeded to the airline counter for our flight to Freeport. We were both excited. We made it on the plane with no problems and flew to Freeport.

It was a small plane and it was a short flight. We got a taxi from the airport that took us to our resort. I think it was the Island Sea Resort. It was beautiful. Right on the beach.

We had a 2 bedroom, 2 bath condo with a living room, full kitchen, balcony, etc. We checked in and decided to go exploring.

We started walking down the road, thinking we would catch a bus. It was a small road, with houses along each side but not right next to each other. We had been walking a while when a van pulled to a stop across the street from us. It was a taxi.

The driver said he would take us into town at Freeport. He said it would be $2.50 each. We also got his phone number if we wanted to go to town again another day.

There are bus stops in town. These were pink and white wood structures. You could wait there and a bus would stop and they would take you back to your resort when you wanted to go back, for the same price. $2.50.

We went to a pretty shopping center and looked around, taking pictures and stopped at "Molly Malones" for happy hour.

There was a sign on the deck outside that read, "Free Husband Sitting - Why not leave him here while you shop. We will take good care of him. Just leave money for his drinks."

We didn't see any husbands, but enjoyed tall cold margaritas. When it was time to head back to our resort, we went to the bus stop and got another cheap ride back.

We were out on the beach and we saw a restaurant/bar a little ways down the beach, so we decided to go there for dinner. It was called Manta Rays.

We walked along the beach to get there. The tide was out so it wasn't a problem. On the way back after dinner we had to walk on the road or get soaked. The tide was in.

The restaurant was open air and there was also seating on the outside deck.

They had torches on the deck that they lit after dark. They had a band and a great menu. We ordered drinks and an entree.

The people there were so nice and all were friendly. It was a beautiful setting right on the beach. We sat on the deck and enjoyed the ocean breeze. We were thrilled with the place.

We could see what looked like a shack, with no walls next door. About 100 feet away. It had a sign that said "Bernie's". It was pretty rustic, not sure what to think about it.

The next day we were walking down the road outside of our resort and a man in an SUV pulled to a stop and gave us his business card. He was the owner, or so we thought, of Bernie's.

He invited us to ride with him to the little shack on the beach. We found out he had drinks, both alcoholic and non-alcoholic and he was the head cook and bottle washer.

He told us what he had on the menu. Barbeque chicken, lobster tails and combination dishes of both. These were served with a salad, and corn on the cob.

He cooked these on an open grill and it smelled wonderful. We decided on the barbeque chicken and thought we would split a meal. The cost was $15.00 a plate.

We ordered a drink and sat on the long bench that was connected to a bar like table of very rustic wood and just enjoyed the ocean breeze while having a cold beer and visited with Bernie as he prepared our meal.

The top of the open air structure had a tarp like cover. It looked like it had been affected by a hurricane recently. We loved it.

It didn't take long and Bernie served our lunch. It was delicious and the servings were very generous. We were glad we split a plate. It was a lot of food.

We watched the sunset while looking out on the white sandy beach. Bernie told us on Tuesdays he had a bonfire there and we should come back.

Several other tourists from the area had joined us and we all had a great time, eating delicious barbeque, talking and sharing stories.

That evening was jazz night at Manta Rays so we decided to go there and had appetizers and listened to the band. We weren't that hungry after having lunch at Bernie's.

At Manta Ray's, there was a cute sign on the outdoor restroom/changing room. "Changing Room Free, to watch $2.00".

We went to the on site restaurant for breakfast the next morning and we spent Monday afternoon laying out on the beach.

We took a tour the next day and went to Gold Rock Beach which was in the Lucayan National Park. The beaches were beautiful white sands with palm trees. We waded in the water, took pictures and just enjoyed the ocean breeze. We were in heaven.

The following day we went for a tour of a neighboring resort and got our bribes. We were to go parasailing and get a massage. Turns out, it was too windy to parasail, so we went for the massage.

After the massage we crossed the street to a beautiful private beach. Other than two other ladies, we had the beach to ourselves.

I hadn't changed into my bathing suit so I borrowed Rebecca's cover up and took off my clothes and put on my bathing suit while wearing her cover up. Nobody was around but I was covered the entire time anyway.

We laid out, took pictures and enjoyed a little bit of heaven...again.

Our days were leisurely and our nights were filled with good food, music and wonderful nights on the beach.

We actually went to game night at our resort one evening and won prizes. We visited with other tourist at our resort and had a lot of laughs.

It was time to go home. We called a taxi to take us to the airport early Saturday morning.

We flew to Nassau and checked our luggage and took a taxi to town. It was about a twenty minute ride.

We went in a fast food restaurant, Burger King and had breakfast. We then started walking. We stopped for pictures whenever we saw something interesting and finally got to the bridge to Paradise Island.

We took a taxi over the bridge and went to Atlantis. The beach and resort was beautiful. More pictures.

At the end of the day we got a taxi back to the airport and caught our flight to the U.S. Our vacation was almost over. What a great trip.

CHAPTER NINETEEN

Myrtle Beach – Let's Shag!

Staying on the beach in December. It was beautiful. I wasn't planning on going in the water or laying out so a winter beach trip was just what I wanted.

I might even check out some property or a condo on the beach. I went on AFVC and rented a cute 1 bedroom condo right on the beach for $349 for 7 days.

I was going there to enjoy the view of the beach, take in a little dancing (learn to shag) and see the local sights.

I'd never been there, so it seemed like a good idea.

When I arrived I took a seat in the airport and went online to rent a car. I couldn't find a good rate before I left home so thought I would try again on arrival.

I got a deal! It was a new SUV with very few miles on it and the rate was close to $100. Right in my budget.

I picked up my car and put the address to my resort in my phone and made it there in around twenty minutes. I checked in and unloaded my luggage.

I was thrilled to see the location and the decor of my condo. It was decorated in light beach colors, Rattan furniture, floral design and stripe fabric cushions, the table was set with matching placemats, napkins and dishes. So cute.

The bedroom was decorated in coordinating colors and the prints on the walls in both rooms were beach scenes. I loved it!

First thing, I opened my sliding door to the balcony and listened to the surf. I was going to love this for seven days.

After unpacking I made my usual trip to the Dollar Tree and picked up supplies to have in the condo.

It was December and cold, so I got what I needed to make a pot of homemade vegetable soup, and a package of cornbread mix. Yum. Perfect for the winter weather.

The kitchen was fully equipped of course, so I knew utensils would not be a problem. I will cook the soup and cornbread tomorrow.

I got ready for the evening out and took off towards North Myrtle Beach. I stopped at a Mexican restaurant along the way. There were tons of restaurants, bars, stores, and shopping on the main drag from Myrtle Beach to North Myrtle Beach.

When I got to North Myrtle Beach I saw a dance club in a small strip mall. There was a band advertised out front so I went in. I was delighted to find most of the clientele was around my age. As it turned out it was "oldies" night. I was referring to the music but you could be referring to the crowd too.

They were swing dancing and seemed to be a friendly group. I got a seat at the bar and watched. It wasn't long before I was asked to dance. I met a couple and they seemed to be dancing with everyone so it wasn't awkward when the husband asked me to dance.

Once you get the first dance, it is not unusual to get asked quite a bit after that. If you can dance. I "can" dance so I was asked to dance many dances. It was a lot fun.

I had contacted two or three gentlemen in the area on a dating website I was on before I left Little Rock.

The next day I met one of them, Archie, at a local restaurant and we had a three hour lunch.

I learned he had moved there from New Jersey because the cost of living was so much better than New Jersey. He told me the real estate taxes were less than half of what he paid in New Jersey.

Did I tell you I was thinking of moving to the beach? I was looking around at Myrtle Beach. It was a real possibility.

Lots of transplants from up North had migrated to the area because of the cost of living being so attractive for retirees and there was a huge dance community. That was a real plus for me. I love to ballroom dance, swing, and country dance and was looking forward to learning the "Shag".

The next day I went out for lunch with another gentleman I met online. We drove over to Murrells Inlet, about twenty miles to a neighboring waterfront town and went to a place called "The Dead Dog Saloon".

We had a delicious lunch and walked along the water on a boardwalk. It was a beautiful view and it was a pretty day, not too cold.

There were lots of plaques along the way on the dock- like structure with names of former patrons. It was fun to read all the plaques and see where the people were from.

After our walk, I checked out the T-Shirts in the gift shop at the "Dead Dog". They had some unique designs.

It was a nice afternoon and my lunch companion was lots of fun even though I didn't fall in love. Lol

It was a nice date. Just so you know. I never expect to fall in love on a date from online dating. I just expect to meet nice people and have a pleasant experience.

That night I went to North Myrtle Beach again, but this time I had looked up a club that offered free "Shag" lessons. It was called Fat Harold's Beach club.

It was a beachy-themed club featuring dancing, DJ's, live music with dance competitions and free Shag lessons. I went in and discovered they offered both a basic and an advanced class. I didn't think I would have trouble in the advanced class, since I had been dancing since I was 9 years old, but thought first things first.

I went to the basic class. I discovered the Shag was very similar to the swing or jitterbug. It only took a few minutes to see that I would "cut my throat" if I had to stay in that very basic class.

They weren't teaching anything that I hadn't known for years. So, I very discreetly told the instructor that I wanted to go to the advanced class.

Not a problem. Until I went in the class! The class was being taught by a young man, but his grandmother was assisting. Not sure why, because the young man was an excellent instructor except she appeared to be a bit of a "control freak".

The grandmother was "old school" and said you "must" count out loud if you were going to take that class. Seriously?

Unless I am teaching someone to dance, "I don't count out loud". She even called me out in front of the class a couple of times because I wasn't counting out loud.

I think it hacked her off that I left the basic class after only a few minutes.

I wasn't having any trouble keeping up or following my partner. I had to bite my tongue on several occasions, but stuck it out.

As usual, when there is a dance class, there is dancing afterward to practice what you learned. A pretty good shag dancer kept asking me to dance. It was good practice but he dominated my dances.

After a couple of hours I decided to go another dance club across the street. This was called "The Duck's Beach Club".

It had a live band, so even if I didn't get asked to dance, I could listen to some good music. As a rule, when you are new to a dance club, particularly country dance clubs, there is a regular crowd, a clique, and you might not get asked to dance if they don't know you.

All of these clubs catered to an older crowd so I thought that would be lots of fun, not competing with young girls, young enough to be my granddaughters.

I hadn't been in the second club very long when the same guy from "Fat Harolds" came in. Grrr. I just wanted to dance with others. Oh well. I got to dance a lot.

When I got tired of watching the women dance "too close" to the men, I decided it was time to leave. The crowds would always start drinking more and start getting friendlier on the dance floor. You know the song "The girls get prettier at closing time"?

I only have one beer when I go out, not only because I am not a heavy drinker but because I was driving.

I rarely dance slow dances, and especially not with strangers. If I do there will be plenty of "air" between us. I am certainly not going to "belly rub" with a total stranger. All in all it was a fun and interesting evening. Another experience.

I woke up early and decided to put on that pot of soup. I enjoyed the view and sound of the surf from my condo. I would crack the sliding door so I could hear it.

I looked on Groupon and saw they had an evening in a local park called "Nights of a Thousand Candles". The event would be open for twelve days. You would see "Brookgreen Gardens" come to life amid the soft glow of more than 4,500 hand-lit candles and countless sparkling lights.

I called Archie to ask if he would like to go. He said "yes", so I picked him up and we headed to Brookgreen Gardens. We were dressed in winter attire, so the weather was cold but tolerable.

There were stations along the paths with warm cider, hot chocolate, holiday music, and carolers singing.

The perfect evening to get in the holiday spirit. We of course took pictures of each other among the candles and lights. Myrtle Beach was turning out to be a good decision.

The next day I went on Groupon and bought a massage. The massage parlor wasn't hard to find and I went through a beautiful community of houses and condos that looked like they should be on the beach.

They were painted in all light pastel colors, had porches and decks, lots of windows, and were on narrow streets. It looked like something out of Disneyworld main street. I got an hour of a relaxing massage for $35 plus tip.

I didn't go to Myrtle Beach to cook. So with the exception of the pot of soup, all my meals were taken at lots of area restaurants. Steak houses, Mexican Restaurants, upscale restaurants featuring great burgers, etc. I can't remember all the names.

I know they were higher priced than what I was accustomed to, but they were in a beach town even if it was off season. You would think it would be cheaper then, but that wasn't the case.

I rarely eat at fast food restaurants or restaurants I can go to at home. I want to experience new things and places when traveling whenever possible.

McDonalds and Burger King were rarely places I visited when traveling.

My last night in Myrtle Beach, my New Jersey friend, Archie, asked me to go to "Broadway at the Beach". It was a beautiful outdoor mall surrounding a small lake.

It was decorated for Christmas and Christmas Music was playing in the piped in system that you could hear while walking around the shopping center.

They had a couple of rides, ferris wheel, boat rides and a "Ripley's Believe It or Not" museum on the property.

I expected crowds of shoppers, as it was December. It was surprisingly quiet. If that place was in Little Rock, it would have been packed.

There was quite a variety of unique shops, but my favorite was a huge shop with candy and treats that were popular in the 50's and 60's. Retro candy. It was called IT'SUGAR. It had things like candy, novelties and gifts.

I loved looking at all the candy that we called "penny candy" when I was growing up, because it was sold for a penny each. A candy bar (Snickers for instance) when I was growing up was a nickel and now you pay a minimum of 89 cents for that same candy bar at a discount store, more if you get it out of a machine. (I know, and "a loaf of bread was 12 cents). But it was!

Do you remember Root Beer Barrels, Sugar Babies, Necco's, Bazooka Gum, Atomic Fireballs, Black Taffy, Dum Dums, Hot Tamales, JuJuBes, Big Hunk, Candy Cigarettes, Boston Baked Beans, Good and Plenty, Wax Lips and Mustaches, Red Hots, Candy necklaces and so many more? It was a fun trip down memory lane.

We ended the evening by me dropping Archie off at his condo, and me giving him a couple of containers of my home made soup in containers I purchased at the Dollar Tree. (I love that store)

I was packed and ready to return home. On the way to the airport I stopped at a huge souvenir shop and purchased my usual. Magnets, a coffee mug and T-Shirts.

I returned my very nice rental car and checked in for my flight.

At the airport I met a lovely older lady that spent part of her time in Myrtle Beach and part of her time in Memphis, Tennessee. We had a nice visit, shared personal stories and exchanged contact information before getting on the plane.

I left Myrtle Beach after a fun filled week and a very nice impression of that part of the country.

CHAPTER TWENTY
10 Day Southern Caribbean Cruise on RCCL

I booked a Royal Caribbean Cruise for a ten day cruise to the Southern Caribbean. I hadn't been to the majority of the ports so I was excited about the different itinerary. I was going to be traveling alone so I checked out their studio cabins. I had seen them online and they were small but so cute. I thought this would be a fun experience and you don't spend much time in your cabin anyway. So I booked my cruise.

Next was my flight. The cruise originated in San Juan, Puerto Rico and returned to San Juan. I got a reasonably priced flight, around $400 round trip.

I learned a lesson on my Mediterranean Cruise, to book a few days before and after and make the most of the cost of flying. I booked my fight three days before my cruise and four days after so I could enjoy San Juan and extend my trip.

I booked my hotel in Bayamon, a neighboring city, because the hotels were more reasonable and I would get to experience a different part of Puerto Rico. I had been to San Juan numerous times on cruises and had seen all of "old San Juan" that I really wanted to see.

I had taken various tours of San Juan over the years. This was to be something different. I went on Hotels.com and booked the Hyatt Place in Bayamon for all seven days of my stay.

The hotel was very nice and my room was great. The room and bathroom was large, I had a comfy king size bed and a view of the pool below. I was on the 6th floor. They had a lovely free breakfast buffet so those meals were taken care of.

I arrived in the afternoon, and after getting all settled in, I decided to go out to dinner. I called an Uber. I found out that Uber's were not allowed to pick up passengers on the hotel grounds but there was a Casino/Restaurant next door that they were allowed to go to. I went next door to wait.

I went to a Spanish, not Mexican Restaurant. I had a delicious dinner and a Margarita. I called an Uber to take me back to my hotel afterwards.

I decided to see what entertainment was in the next door Casino. There was a live band in one of the bars so I found a seat and enjoyed "people watching" while listening to the music.

The second day I decided to take the train in to San Juan. The station was just a short distance so I hopped on a city bus.

There was a bus stop in front of my hotel and I always loved riding on the train. It was fun to see all the people that rode the train to work and back or to who knows where. They appeared to be from all walks of life. It was easy, inexpensive transportation.

I got off the train in downtown San Juan and started walking around the town, taking pictures, looking in shops, purchasing souvenirs and just enjoying the beautiful weather.

I ended up at the Harbor and saw a Mexican Restaurant right on the water and decided that would be a good place to have a late lunch. The service was excellent and the food was reasonably priced and delicious.

I left the restaurant and saw some vendors outside. A cruise ship had pulled into port and passengers were disembarking the ship, so it was a perfect place to sell their wares. I purchased a bracelet.

When it was starting to get dark, I decided to take the train back to Bayamon. When I got to the station in Bayamon I thought I would catch a bus back to my hotel. I waited, and waited and finally someone told me buses didn't run that late. Oops.

I started walking and started looking around and what did I discover? My hotel was just a block away. I guess I took a circle trip when I took the bus "from" the hotel earlier in the day to the train station. So....I walked. I had to laugh at my ignorance.

On the way back to my hotel I noticed a large mall. I decided to stop in and see what stores were there. I saw they had a movie theater so I bought a ticket and watched a movie. Thank God it was in English, although the previews were not. After the movie, I walked around the corner to my hotel.

The next morning I decided to go to the Bacardi Rum Plant and take a tour. It is the largest premium rum distillery in the world.

I took an Uber and the first thing we got after purchasing a ticket was a Daiquiri, with rum of course. It was included in the tour price.

We then hopped on a Tram that held about 15 people and toured the property and saw and heard how the rum was made. Several rooms had pictures and videos showing the process. The tour ended in a gift shop where you could buy a variety of rum, gifts and souvenirs. It was an interesting tour.

After the tour I had an Uber drop me off at the Mall of San Juan. It was the most beautiful three story mall covering 650,000 square feet. It had everything from Armani, Coach, Bulgari, Gucci, and Louis Vuitton to Saks Fifth Avenue and Banana Republic. It is considered to be world-class shopping and is San Juan's premier shopping destination. The number of stores and services is 100.

I'm not a shopper just to shop and certainly didn't shop at designer stores that were in that mall. I did find a costume jewelry shop and they were having a half price sale.

Back in Chapter 4 I told you my jewelry had been stolen from my luggage. I had been reimbursed so I decided to replenish my jewelry collection. I purchased a few things at full price but most were selected at 50% off.

I was having a blast picking out pieces in all colors and designs. Hopefully they would fit in my carry-on and not be a problem adding to the weight of my luggage. I was going to be traveling for 15 days and this was just the beginning of my trip.

The next day and the reason for my visit to San Juan was my 12 day cruise to the Southern Caribbean. The ports for the most part, were places I had never visited. I had also never been to so many ports in almost as many days. Too many for my taste really. I usually enjoy the days at sea more than anything else.

The hotel shuttle driver dropped me off in San Juan at the pier. That was extremely kind of him as a private car or shuttle from Bayamon would have been expensive.

I got to the port where the Adventures of the Sea was docked. It was a beautiful ship both inside and out. The check in process was pretty quick even though I had no priority privileges with Royal Caribbean.

When we boarded I started looking for my room. I think my cabin was on the third floor. It was difficult to find as it was in a secluded part of the ship. It was separated by a desk with two doors going into hallways with cabins on each side. I was at the end of a small hallway.

When I opened my door was I in for a shock. The cabin was nothing like those cute little rooms on the website. I think they had converted a closet to make my room. They were new rooms, but that was the only plus.

It only took a minute to look around the room. I had been on 28 cruises before this one and this was the smallest and worst room I had ever had. It was also the most expensive.

I paid more for this room than a balcony cabin at peak sailing dates on Carnival. I also paid more for it than my Alaskan cruise for my son and myself, and it was on the Rhapsody of the Seas, another Royal Caribbean Ship.

I immediately went to the Guest Services Desk to see if I could be moved or upgraded. I was told the entire ship was booked and no other rooms were available. I was not a happy camper, to say the least.

That will be my last Royal Caribbean Cruise. Later I met my friend Jane and learned that she had booked the same type room but was able to see an actual picture before the cruise and got an upgrade for $50. She got an Ocean View Cabin that was exactly like the cabins I usually got on Carnival. If you think I wasn't happy before, you can imagine how I felt about my closet of a room after that.

The bed in my cabin looked and felt like a rollaway bed, there were no pictures on the wall and a desk with a TV monitor instead of a vanity where you could sit in front of a mirror and apply your make-up. The only mirror was a wall mirror and one over the sink in the bathroom. You could sit at the end of my bed and take one step and be in the bathroom. How convenient!

One day I ordered room service and the waiter just looked around trying to figure out where he could set the tray. No coffee table, no bedside table, no place on the desk with the monitor, nothing! He had to set the tray on the bed. Some luxury cruise this was. Not!

Our first stop was St. Thomas in the U.S. Virgin Islands. I had been there several times on other cruises. I was familiar with the shuttles, shopping areas, flea markets and restaurants. I took a shuttle with several other passengers for about $8.00.

It was a nice day and I found some T-shirts, a knock off Coach purse for my daughter-in-law and just looked around at the local shops.

On my return to the ship there was a small bar at the port, really an open air hut like bar. The beer was $3, which was a bargain compared to the prices on the ship.

I sat down and had a beer and met two very nice (and nice looking) guys. We were sharing where we came from and they said "they were on their honeymoon" and showed me their wedding pictures. They had a huge wedding with 200 guests, music, a beautiful wedding cake with two grooms on top and seemed to be so happy. My luck, I meet two good looking guys and "they" are married. To each other no less.

We had a great time visiting, running into each other on the ship, getting our pictures taken together. They were the nicest, friendliest people I met on that whole cruise.

I forgot to tell you. There were over 3,000 passengers and my friend Jane and I appeared to be the only ones that weren't part of a couple! No singles!

We went to one singles gathering and Jane and I were the only ones to show up. I went out on the deck to look out on the water and look at the moon. A few minutes later a single guy about 35 walked up and started a conversation with me. We talked and took a seat by the closed bar on deck and just got to know each other.

He was definitely too young, but a nice kid. My co-workers and family would always ask me if I got married when I returned from a cruise. They all have seen Love Boat too many times. That does not happen even if there are singles on board. Usually people travel in pairs on cruises because the cost of one is like paying for two passengers. The odds of meeting someone and falling in love are pretty much non existent.

If you are in your 20's, 30's or 40's you might meet someone to "hook-up" with, but after the cruise or after that night, you are forgotten. Shipboard romances are designed to be just that. While you are "on board". I have known people that have had those experiences, but before you think I am speaking from personal experience, it never happened to me.

The third day was Barbados. Jane and I got a tour from the dock and saw the island with a very informative tour guide in a van with four of us in the van. The couple with us hadn't eaten breakfast and were looking for a quick place to stop and grab something on the go for lunch. The driver pulled up to a house and told the young lady to go up to the door and tell the lady of the house that Cecil sent her. She did that and came back with a plate of food that was home cooked on a real plate with a silver fork.

Cecil told us that his mother lived in that house and did catering and always had food prepared. Our tour partner got a home cooked meal and it was free. Wow!

We toured the whole Island and made several stops along the way, to include the beach. We were going back to the ship. When we had left the tour van, Jane realized she had left her Iphone in the van. We tried to find Cecil and knew he worked at the shipyard at night. He was going home to change clothes before his shift started later that afternoon. Jane was frantic. I would be too.

We only had a little over an hour before our ship would be sailing. I wasn't about to miss the ship so Jane took off in search of Cecil. She was finally able to reach him through people at the dock and he brought her the phone. She made it back just in time to board before the ship was to sail. Whew. That was a close one.

The following day was our first day at sea. I was ready for a sea day. I laid out in the sun, sat in the hot tub and just had a relaxing day.

That night we had a lovely dinner and went to an ice skating show. Yes an ice skating show on the ship. The skaters were all very attractive, the costumes were beautiful and we had a wonderful time.

Tuesday was Bonaire, followed by Antigua and St. Lucia. Three stops that didn't impress me. These places were very primitive and also expensive.

Jane snorkeled at almost every port. I am not one to swim with "critters", so I took land tours. Souvenirs were very expensive. They didn't have anything I couldn't live without.

Finally we arrived in Curacao. It was beautiful and my favorite port.

I took a tour of the city and I was pleasantly surprised by how nice it was. We were told that so many places in the city had been painted in the pretty pastels because the Mayor of the City had a relative in the paint business. I don't know if that was true or not.

The shopping in Curacao was great. Prices were reasonable and I found a tote bag, beach dresses for my former co-worker and daughter-in-law and magnets for Tammy, a mug for Matt and T-shirts. Yay.

The weather was wonderful and there were lots of places to get some great pictures. I was tired of walking so I decided to go to one of the bars in the area that attracted tourists to just sit and have a cool drink.

The bartenders were very friendly so we talked, took pictures and just had a good time till it was time for me to go back to the ship. I absolutely loved Curacao.

The next and last port was Aruba. I was really looking forward to Aruba. I had heard so much about it. It sounded so beautiful, tropical and exotic in songs and in travel brochures.

I took a tour with a lady I had met on the cruise. Her husband wanted to snorkel and she wanted to tour the city, so we got on a tour bus that took us to beautiful beaches and up in the hills to a lighthouse, a small chapel and lots of nice homes.

I was surprised that if you weren't on the beach, it looked like a desert with cactus, dry dirt fields and you would think you were in Arizona. I was shocked. I guess if you just stayed on the beach or at a resort, it would be a beautiful visit.

We finished the tour and hit the shops to pick up a few souvenirs, took more pictures and then walked back to the ship.

Our last day was at sea and then back to San Juan. The week was filled with taking dance classes, going to shows, having wonderful dinners and just relaxing on the ship between all those ports.

We arrived in San Juan on Saturday and I went back to the Hilton Place in Bayamon to spend a few more days before flying home. I spent time shopping, going to another movie, getting my nails done, my hair done, dining out and just having a good time.

CHAPTER TWENTY-ONE
Breaking Out of Rehab

Let me clarify this. I wasn't in Rehab. My dear friend JoAnn was and had been in a facility for two years when I asked her if she would like to go on a cruise. She said yes, and was thrilled about it.

I booked a 7 day cruise for the two of us on the Carnival Breeze out of Galveston. Then the planning started.

I booked a hotel for the night before our cruise in Galveston at the Beachcomber Inn on Hotels.com. Not a fancy hotel but okay for a night. It was clean and close to restaurants and a couple of blocks from the beach. The plus for choosing that hotel was they provided free cruise parking. Yay!

I started shopping and borrowing clothes for JoAnn because cruise attire and rehab attire are totally different. I was having a ball doing all this and getting more excited as the cruise date was getting closer.

One day JoAnn called me and said "this is the hardest call I've ever had to make." She said because her room/bed was a medicare bed, she was not allowed to leave the country and would not be able to go on the cruise.

I was sad for her and me. This would have been her first cruise, and would be something she would never forget. Not to mention a great break from sitting in that room that was no bigger than a jail cell.

Her life consisted of watching TV, playing on her laptop, Facebook and visiting with her many friends and family as well as counseling the young nurses and aides.

JoAnn was one of the sweetest people I have ever met and had a personality that was fun for everybody she met. Like me, she never met a stranger.

I think she provided the most comic relief for the staff in the nursing facility as well as for me. We talked daily. Most of the times more than once a day.

Twenty five years prior to the scheduled cruise, JoAnn and I met when I was a Human Resources Specialist for Metlife and was interviewing her for a job.

She had recently moved to Little Rock from Newport, Arkansas. I asked her why she left her last job. She had managed the Country Club for eleven years. She told me she married a member of the club and the board of directors thought that would be a conflict of interest.

After her termination, she and her husband worked in Real Estate together and were very happy. Six months after they married, her husband dropped dead of a heart attack.

JoAnn and I had similar backgrounds, although I didn't ever live in a small town or have a husband to die after six months of marriage.

After her first marriage ended, she had two boys to raise. Her sons were only a couple of years difference in age. She did it alone and they were her whole life. There was nothing JoAnn wouldn't do for her boys.

After that first phone call from Joann cancelling the cruise, I said to her "well if you can't leave the country why don't we go to Branson and stay at a resort for a week. We can go to a couple of shows, dine out, lay by the pool and just have a fun relaxing week".

She agreed that would be fun so I booked a resort for 7 days. A two bedroom, two bath Condo for $349 through AFVC. She wouldn't need formal wear but the clothes I had already bought for her for the cruise could still be used.

I was trying to muster up some excitement even though Branson wasn't my favorite place to go for a week. JoAnn and I could have fun staying home, so I knew we could have a great time anywhere we went.

We were all set, and then I get another phone call from JoAnn. She said the rehab facility said she couldn't go. I was having a hard time with this so I called the rehab facility myself only to learn that it wasn't their decision but JoAnn's son Brians.

I decided to call Brian. I asked him if there was some reason he didn't want his Mom to go on a trip with me. I had known Brian for twenty years and he knew JoAnn and I were the best of friends.

He said, "yes there most certainly is". I was floored and asked what that reason was. He said, "I am not going to let her do anything that will get her back in the place she was two years ago."

Her reason for being in the rehab was for depression and early onset Dementia or so they thought. In fact it was a change in her medication and it took a year to get her back to normal, finally getting her medication right.

JoAnn was back to "the old JoAnn" and that was the reason I had asked her to go on a trip. I had my friend back. We were all thrilled that she was the old Joann again.

I said to Brian, "you can't possibly think I would do anything that would hurt JoAnn. I love her like a sister. " He said she still couldn't go. I was so upset that I needed to hang up the phone before I said something I would regret.

So here I am with two trips that I had paid for that were totally non-refundable. What do I do?

I sent a text to my friend Rebecca and told her she had just won an all expense paid 7 day cruise. She sent me a text back and said she thought my phone had been hacked. I said no it hadn't and asked if she wanted to go. Her answer was yes yes yes yes! Maybe even a couple of more yes's.

I checked with Carnival and I just had to pay another deposit. I only lost $50, as Carnival gave me back the remainder of my initial deposit as a future on board credit. So I wouldn't lose it all, it would just be available on a future cruise.

Rebecca was excited and so was I. It was Rebecca's first cruise and I was thrilled she was going. It is always fun to share a vacation with a first time cruiser.

Well I solved one problem, but I still had a week in Branson all paid for and nobody to go with me. I called my friend and dance partner Jon, and asked if he would like to go. He said of course. I told him the condo was paid for already. He said he would take care of our meals. That worked!

I had already booked a trip to Las Vegas the week before our Branson trip. I wouldn't be returning till the Saturday we were to leave to drive to Branson.

Luckily, I had a washer and dryer at my condo in Las Vegas, so I did laundry so I would have clean clothes for the next week in Branson.

Jon picked me up at the Little Rock Airport around 2 p.m. and we drove to Branson. We checked in to the condo in Branson around 7 p.m. We stopped on the way at a small Italian restaurant near Harrison and had dinner.

When we got to the Surrey Vacation Resort, I claimed the master bedroom. Was that tacky of me? It had a king size bed, a jacuzzi tub and enough room to dance the waltz in between the bed and the vanity. It was wonderful.

Jon got the bedroom up front in the condo, and he had his own bathroom, although it wasn't in his bedroom. It was all very nice even if it wasn't the larger of the two rooms.

The condo had a full kitchen, dining area and living room. Each room had a TV. So we had three TV's. Definitely all the comforts of home.

We took our luggage in and then made a trip to Walmart to buy a few supplies for the condo. Breakfast food, juice, snacks and soft drinks. We would not be cooking that week.

We went to a couple of shows. One was a fifties show and was great. I got tickets on Groupon of course.

We had lunch at Mel's Hard Luck Diner. It was a 50's diner atmosphere and the waiters and waitresses serenade their guests throughout the day.

Mel's specializes in great food, great music, and a unique and memorable experience. A lovely restaurant where the waiters and waitress would sing while you were having your meal.

Mel's is located in the Shops at Grand Village. After dining at Mel's we had to look in the many cool and unique shops at the Grand Village and pick up a souvenir or two.

Jon and I went to Inspiration Tower and went to the top for the view. When returning to the ground floor we were approached by a young lady and she swayed us to take a tour of an area lake community. It was a lovely area and Jon thought it might be a good investment for one of his family members.

Although they didn't call them bribes in the U.S., they offered gifts in exchange for the time we spent on the tour. We spent a very pleasant 55 minute tour and the sales people sent us on our way. We went by the office near Branson's Landing and collected our gifts. We got a gift card from Walmart, a free Mexican dinner for two and $50 in cash.

That evening we went to the Chateau on the Lake Resort for dinner and enjoyed the lakeview dining. After dinner we sat out on the deck and watched the sun go down. It was a beautiful restaurant and the view after dinner was just as pleasant as the fine dining.

The following day we decided to take a drive to Eureka Springs. The road to Eureka was winding and two lane so I was white knuckling it all the way over and back. We walked among the shops, picked up a souvenir or two and had lunch in downtown Eureka Springs.

We hadn't made it to Branson Landing yet so we took off to visit there the next day. We went down on the main drag and visited the five and dime store and picked up a couple of toys for the grandkids that were popular in the fifties.

We saw a victorian shop and I wanted to go in. I fell in love with the place. I got this bright idea of redecorating my bedroom in this style so I picked out two frilly lamp shades. They were ridiculously priced, but I bought them and had them packed in a box so they would make the trip home without any damage.

We then went to Branson Landing, and rode on Parakeet Pete's Steampunk Balloon. It was a hot air balloon ride that was in a cage like structure that went up like an elevator. The balloon went up 188 feet and you had an amazing view of Lake Taneycomo and the Ozark Mountains. We took pictures, bought a T-Shirt and enjoyed the information that the operator shared with us about the history of the balloon.

We then went to the fountain show at the Landing that was orchestrated to music. We browsed the shops and then left for The Track Family Fun Park.

We rode the go-carts. The track was a spiraling, twisting and turning on a new 4 story steel and concrete track. You got to do the track two times. We acted like kids racing each other and making the sharp turns and going down the steep hills. We had a ball.

The last day we took advantage of our free Mexican Dinner. I touched the hot plate and burnt my fingers. I had never experienced anything like that from a plate that was set in front of me. I was just going to scoot it over. Ouch.

On the way home, I had it on ice. It felt like it was on fire. We stopped at a McDonalds halfway to Little Rock as the ice had melted and it was still burning like crazy. I sat with my fingers in a cup till we drove up to my house.

After four hours on the road it was still burning. I had a difficult time getting my keys out and unlocking my door. Damn, that really hurt.

It was now time for the cruise. Rebecca and I drove to Galveston. Just as we were entering Galveston, Rebecca started tearing up. I asked her what was wrong. She said, "nothing, I just can't believe I'm here and we're actually going on a cruise".

We stayed overnight at the Beachcomber Inn, went out for dinner at a restaurant on the beach and boarded the Carnival Breeze for the 7 day cruise the next morning. We were both excited.

Our cruise took us to Belize, Honduras and Cozumel. We toured each location, shopped and ended it with a wonderful massage in Cozumel. Rebecca had never been to any of those ports and we had a wonderful time.

All week people would ask if we were sisters. We decided to have some fun and just say we were mother/daughter. We are both blondes so they bought that story, hook, line and sinker.

Rebecca is the same age as my oldest son, so that seemed more believable to us too.

We drove back to Little Rock with lots of pictures, souvenirs and many happy memories of a great cruise. I made an album for Rebecca of all of our cruise pictures and surprised her with it a week after we returned from our trip.

We've cruised again and made two other trips together since then. I still tell people she's my daughter.

CHAPTER TWENTY-TWO
Free Week in Mazatlan

Usually in Mexico you got exceptional maid service. This resort was no exception. I would come back at the end of the day to find towel animals in the bathroom, on the bed and on the kitchen counter. My maid "Maria" was so sweet and thoughtful. When I left the resort I left Maria a Thank you note with a nice tip.

As a result of going to a sales pitch at the property in Panama City, Florida I was given a free week at a resort of my choice. I hadn't been to Mazatlan in several years so I thought it would be fun to revisit.

I looked online at their inventory that looked like the AFVC site. I found a very attractive resort available the week I was interested in going.

I started looking for a flight next. I found one within my budget of between $300 and $400.

I don't usually rent a car in Mexico because the cars are cheap, but the insurance is outrageous and my insurance in the states doesn't cover Mexico. Public transportation in Mexico is ridiculously cheap and convenient enough, so my plan was to use the bus system or taxi's.

I went to the pool to have lunch and wait until the check-in time.

I arrived in the early afternoon and check-in wasn't until 4:00 p.m. I finally made it to ny condo. It was beautiful. It had a full kitchen, living room, big bedroom and separate bathroom and dressing area. The ceilings were at least 10 ft. so that gave it the appearance of being even larger than it actually was. Wall to wall full length windows with sliding doors to the balcony in both the living room and bedroom with a view of the pool and the ocean. Not bad for a free week.

I checked with the Concierge desk and asked if he knew of a good place to have dinner that also had live music. It was Sunday night and I didn't know what to expect. He told me of a place called "La Katrina". It was a few miles from the resort but the city bus would go right in front of it.

There was a bus stop in front of my resort so I decided to take the bus instead of a taxi. The bus fare was 20 pesos or a dollar in U.S money.

It wasn't long before I saw the restaurant. We were almost passed it when I spotted it, so by the time we stopped I had to walk back about a block. It was a beautiful evening. Not too hot and definitely not too cold. The walk was pleasant.

When I got to La Katrina I discovered it had a nice crowd and to my surprise and delight, the music was not your typical Mariachi Band but "Country Music". I love country music but that was the last thing I expected to hear.

I found a seat at the large bar that circled the center of the room. Tables and chairs were on the perimeter and covered the entire area of a large room. The band was near the entrance.

The band leader asked if there was anybody there from the U.S. and a handful of people yelled out and clapped. He then asked if there were any Canadians and the whole place erupted with yells and applause. Wow! I had no idea it was such a popular place for the Canadians.

I later found out that many Canadians lived there anywhere from three to six months to get away from the bitter cold winters of Canada. I don't blame them, I would go South too.

I looked over the menu and ordered a chicken sandwich. They brought me a huge fried chicken sandwich with fries. It was ridiculously inexpensive. About six U.S. dollars.

A gentleman, Murray, sitting next to me struck up a conversation with me and I learned he was one of the many Canadians. Murray was a dairy farmer.

He was traveling solo and was only going to be there for a week too so we talked about things we were going to do. We decided to get acquainted with the area together.

Not too many minutes later, an "older than me" lady sat down next to me. I introduced myself and Murray. We were all three traveling solo. Her name was Irene. Irene was also from Canada and told us she had been spending the winter months in Mazatlan for years.

There were several televisions scattered around the bar. The station was tuned to a sport called Curling. Both Murray and Irene were familiar with the game and explained it to me. It is apparently very popular in Canada.

The next morning I decided to take a bus to town. I thought La Katrina's was "in" town. The city was quite a bus ride from La Katrina's but the fare was the same.

I got off the bus where lots of other riders got off, in the city center. There was a square with a large elevated gazebo in the middle of it with lots of trees and greenery. There were park benches were ten or so feet and most were occupied by tourists and people from Mazatlan, young and old.

The Basilica of the Immaculate Conception was across the street, also known as the Mazatlan Cathedral. It was a beautiful cathedral so I took some pictures.

I walked down a couple of blocks and saw a restaurant/bakery called "Panera", which in Spanish translates to "bread box or bread basket". I had seen two other Panera's from the bus and decided to try it for breakfast. It was a busy restaurant.

Half was restaurant and the other half was bakery. I had a delicious omelette with hash browns and toast and then went to the bakery side. The bakery was busy as well.

They had trays like you would use at a cafeteria in the states, and you used long metal tongs to select what you wanted.

They had a huge selection of sweet rolls, danish rolls, mufins, cakes, etc. I selected a couple of muffins and a couple of sweet rolls to have in the condo for breakfast. You would take this to a counter and the clerks would bag it up and give you a ticket showing the content. You would take this to a cashier and they would ring up your purchases. It was a great system. I had a microwave in the condo, so they would be yummy in the mornings without having to go out first thing to get breakfast. I picked up some diet cokes at a local market to have in the condo as well.

I walked around, looking in shops, looking for souvenirs as well as anything else that might strike my fancy. I bought a pair of flats at a bargain.

It was difficult to figure out their sizing because they used European sizing. I discovered I wore a size 39-40 which would equate to a U.S. size 9. I found that the most popular or plentiful sizes in Mexico was a 6-7.5 or 36.5 to 38. I think my size is about average (maybe) in the U.S. In Mexico it is large.

In the early afternoon I stopped at a sidewalk cafe and had Fajitas for lunch. They were delicious. There was a small square in front of the restaurant. People would walk their dogs, visit with others and sit on one of the benches and enjoy the sunlight.

Street vendors would approach tourist trying to sell their merchandise. Silver is a popular item being sold all over Mexico. I was approached by one of these vendors and bargained for one of his silver bracelets. I bought one and and still wear it almost daily.

That evening I went back to La Katrina's and met up with Murray. We had dinner together and listened to the band.

Neither of us had been to an island we had heard about so our plan was to meet for breakfast the next morning and head out there for the day. The island was called Stone Island.

We took what they call a Pulmonia. This is a "golf cart" type vehicle that was open air with a canvas top that resembles a "surrey with the fringe on top". They can usually hold 2-4 passengers.

Another mode of public transportation is an Aurigas. They are pickup trucks with benches and a cover over the back (or bed) of the truck. Prices on both of these vehicles are negotiable The price should be decided before you start the ride.

The Pulmonias and the Aurigas are priced per ride, not per passenger. The Aurigas can hold up to 8 to 12 people so it is very economical for groups. The Aurigas usually have loud music playing which adds to a party atmosphere in the open air ride.

When we made it to the ferry, we learned it was not the large ferry but really a motor boat about a block away. We went there and purchased a ticket and got in the boat. It was only maybe a ten minute ride to get to the Island.

Upon arrival we were approached by a man on the beach with an Iguana. The Iguana was about 3 feet long. The Iguana's owner said we could pet or hold it, I declined. eeeeew.

I did take pictures. The man would touch or tickle the Iguana under its neck and the Iguana would lift its hand or paw as if he was saying "hi". I am not a fan of Iguana's, snakes or lizards but this Iguana was so cute.

The man had owned this particular Iguana for eleven years, or so he said. There are reports of Iguana's living past 20 years in captivity.

We walked along the beach and saw several open air restaurant/bars sitting right on the beach. We got a table at one and ordered beers and just enjoyed the breeze, the surf and sand. The beach was beautiful.

Mariachi bands and street dancers performed for the tourist on the sand in front of the open air restaurants. Men playing guitars and groups doing acrobatic tricks would stop and entertain the customers too.

We left in the late afternoon and found a path up a small rocky mountain. Murray climbed to the top while I stayed below and took pictures of the rocks, the ocean and the beach. It was a beautiful setting so I took a few selfies.

There were some carpenters building small houses right there on the beach. We wondered what these small houses would sell for. I thought it would be fun to own a small house right on the beach.

The next day I took a bus to where the bus dropped me the day before at the city center. I had an appointment for a massage at a place called The Athena Spa. The massage was in a lovely corner building, with A/C and soft music piped in to the entire facility. I got an hour massage and topped it off with a pedicure. It was wonderful and so relaxing.

After my spa experience I walked back to the square where I saw a huge tent and a group of women doing aerobics to music for breast cancer awareness. I stopped to watch and take pictures.

I finished up my day at an indoor flea market that offered every kind of souvenir you could imagine and and kind of food item you could possibly want.

I took the bus back to my resort and laid out on the beach. The remainder of my days in Mazatlan were spent sunning on the beach or laying out by the pool. Another great trip in Mexico.

CHAPTER TWENTY-THREE

Reno, Nevada – Built In Tour Guide

My niece Andra lives in Reno, but I didn't think we would get to spend more than a day or two together. Much to my delight and surprise, Andra took time out of her very busy life to be my tour guide for the entire week. It was so much fun. Andra's husband works in San Jose and commuted from Reno staying in San Jose for the work week before returning home for the weekend. Andra worked from home and was raising her two teenage sons and providing taxi service to one of her sons job and their many school, sports and church activities.

I hadn't been to Reno, Nevada in over a year so I decided to make that my next trip. I went on AFVC and booked a 1 Bedroom condo with living room, partial kitchen\dining, and bath for my usual $349 a week. The resort was right downtown, so I didn't see the need to rent a car. I would Uber, take busses or walk where I wanted to go.

Upon my arrival I called my niece. I was excited to see her and her family. Andra married her husband Jim, several years before my visit. She had three boys, and he had two daughters and a son, so they blended their families. I was amazed how successful that was.

The kids ranged from two to sixteen. They met and started their marriage in San Jose before they decided to return to Andra's home town. Jim's job was too good to walk away from, so he commuted. Andra also had a great job but she was fortunate enough that she could work from home.

Jim and Andra would talk on the phone as much as possible, skype daily and made the situation work for the sake of all of the family.

Reno is approximately 37 miles from beautiful Lake Tahoe, 26 miles from historic Virginia City, and Carson City the state Capitol of Nevada, was approximately 34 miles away.

I was pleasantly surprised to find out that Andra had planned to spend as much time with me as I wanted and proceeded to be my tour guide. She came into town and we started our visit and sightseeing.

Our first stop was the famous city sign right in the middle of downtown Reno. The sign reads, "Reno - The Biggest Little City in the World". The sign has been featured in lots of movies and was of historical interest in the city.

We walked along the riverwalk that was part of a revitalization program that started in the mid 1990's. It follows the Truckee River that flows through downtown Reno and bisects the town.

The river is a popular spot for kayaking, tubing, and swimming as well as making it a nice spot in the evening to take a stroll along the riverwalk.

Reno has a "sculpture garden" in the Bicentennial Park in an effort to add some extra character to the riverwalk.

We spent most of the first day in downtown Reno. We went to the National Automobile Museum which was one of our first stops. The museum housed more than 220 classic cars.

We visited the National Bowling Stadium which is a 363,000 square ten-pin bowling stadium. The stadium has 78 bowling lanes and houses the Bowling Museum and Hall of Fame.

When you first walk in the museum there is a giant bowling ball and bowling pin. We had our pictures made in front of it and looked small in comparison.

The stadium is recognizable on the outside by an 80 feet aluminum geodesic dome in its facade, built to resemble a large bowling ball. The Hall of Fame houses an impressive display of paintings of the Hall of Fame members.

The Playa Art Park is the home of the Burning Man sculptures. There are eleven Burning Man art pieces in the park.

1. The Space Whale is a life-size sculpture of a mother and calf humpback whale made of steel lattice and custom-designed stained glass.

2. The "Believe" sculpture is one of the many wood sculptures. Each one of the sculptures is 12 foot high, 4 foot thick rustic steel.

3. Portal of Evolution - Better known by some as the "winged sculpture" for the butterfly wings the rotate in the wind.

4. Guardian of Eden - Intricately carved Lotus Petals.

5. Electric - A wooden car sculpture is an homage to the Cadillac Ranch, where ten Cadillacs were buried in the Texas prairie, leaving only the tail fins visible.

6. Starway - Standing over 15 feet tall is a star made of more than 200 individual lit neon stars.

7. Good Luck Horseshoe - 8 foot tall steel horseshoe.

8. Electric Dandelions - A group of three 23 - 27 foot tall dandelion sculptures that look like frozen fireworks at night.

9. Imago - Blue mirror steel butterflies that hover 17 feet above.

10. Reno Star Cosmic Thistle - Stands 46 feet tall and 60 feet wide. The design was inspired by high desert plants found in the Great Basin. Made from repurposed steel from the city of Reno.

11. Ichthyosaur - 50 foot model of Nevada's state fossil. Made of plywood.

The second day we decided to go to Donner Memorial State Park. This was the site of the Donner Camp, where members of the ill-fated Donner Party were trapped by weather during the winter of 1846-1847. Caught without shelter or adequate supplies, members of the group resorted to cannibalism to survive.

Donner Lake is a beautiful lake approximately eleven miles from Lake Tahoe. The entire lake can be viewed from Donner Pass. Elevation of Donner Lake is 5,936 feet.

The third day Andra, Ethan, Tyler and myself drove up the mountain, another white knuckle event, to Virginia City, Nevada.

Virginia City was known as the most important industrial city between Denver and San Francisco in the early 1900's. It was a mining town. We visited saloons, shops and had lunch at the Palace Saloon and Restaurant.

That evening Andra had church so I booked a show at a local casino. I had dinner at the same casino. I caught an Uber to and from the Show. The show was a variety show of Cirque Du Soleil. The show was amazing and was truly artistic and creative.

The fourth day I had booked a massage with a Groupon, The massage parlor was within walking distance, so I took off on foot to find it.

Every massage is different but this one was probably the only one that was disappointing. It was very relaxing if you could just get over the fact her touch was too light. It was almost irritating. I tried to just relax and go with it. Enjoy the moment.

We went to Andra's sons (Ethan) track meet in Carson City that afternoon. He was a freshman in high school and was a pole vaulter.

We watched the competition and cheered for Ethan and his team mates. We were wrapped up in coats and gloves as it was a bit chilly and windy outside.

We drove a little over thirty minutes to get there and we toured the downtown area, saw the State Capitol, and took lots of pictures.

After touring downtown Carson City we went to the school where the track meet was held. The drive to and from Carson City was very scenic and we were surrounded by mountains in the distance.

Our fifth day we went to a shopping mall and rode on an indoor ferris wheel, had lunch at a Mexican restaurant and I got a second piercing in my ears.

I decided to cook a steak dinner for Andra and her family so I went to the store to purchase supplies. Our menu consisted of salad, steak, baked potatoes, baked beans and Hummingbird cake for dessert. I thought it was the least I could do after the hospitality I was shown by Andra and her whole family.

I didn't mention it earlier, but on more than one occasion we would go back to her house in the evening after a day of touring.

It was about a 15 mile drive from my resort so we would have dinner and relax in her hot-tub or listen to the boys play music.

We both talked non-stop. We had so much to say in the short time we would be together. We wanted to make the most of our visit.

My niece was an excellent tour guide, but the best part of the trip was just being able to spend time with her.

Andra is my oldest sister's oldest daughter. She reminded me so much of my sister. Her Mom Linda, passed in 2011 of lung cancer. Andra is my sister made over.

She is talented musically, does every kind of craft, is very artistic and works tirelessly with the young women of her church, while running a household and raising her kids and still holds a successful job.

She is a loving wife, Mom, Aunt and friend. Andra is a wonderful young woman and I love her dearly.

CHAPTER TWENTY-FOUR

The End of My Retirement Trips...NOT!

No this is not the end of my travels. I just wrote about the most memorable trips, or maybe they were just the ones I could remember at the time. I don't ever plan to stop traveling till I take that last trip when my ashes are dropped from a cruise ship.

I might take a short break and finish this book. I have a trip to Las Vegas planned in June and a return trip to Mazatlan in September.

I have two cruises booked at this time. One on the Carnival Horizon in October of this year, a second cruise on the Mardi Gras in October 2020.

The Mardi Gras is going to be the special trip. Our first cruise in 1980 was on Carnival's first ship and it was named the Mardi Gras. (In those days I cruised with my family).

The original Mardi Gras was only a little over 27,000 tons with 958 passengers. We thought it was huge and beautiful. It was a very classy atmosphere even though the ship itself was not nearly as big or as elaborately decorated like the ships these days.

The original Mardi Gras had lots of wood and brass in the interior. The service on any cruise line is the selling point that keeps passengers coming back and the service on the Mardi Gras was fantastic. You didn't have to do anything but sleep and get dressed. Everything else was done for you.

All this is still done on Carnival. Your cabin steward cleans your room twice a day, once when you leave in the morning and once after you leave for your dinner.

You always come back to your room after your evening with your bed turned down and a "towel animal" on the bed with your "Fun Times".

The fun times is a schedule of events for the next day. You always need to refer to it or you will miss an activity or event. It is now on a HUB that can be downloaded on your phone free of charge so you can refer to it.

For a $5.00 charge you have texting available with your fellow passengers on the Hub. This is worth every penny even if you only use it to keep up with your family and cabin mates. You could spend an entire day trying to find each other if you don't decide on a meeting place in advance. The ships are so huge, like a huge floating hotel. The Hub solves that problem of keeping up with each other.

The wait staff in the "fine dining" is and always has been fantastic. They learn your name the first night and always address you by your name, they remember your likes and dislikes and serve you accordingly. I drink iced tea for every meal and after the first night I never had to tell them, they would just serve it.

In the past they had a Captains party. It was a formal night and every passenger had the opportunity to meet the Captain and have their picture taken with him.

At the Captains Party complimentary cocktails and hors d'oeuvres were served, the ships orchestra played dance music and the passengers were invited to dance on the stage during the party. The Captain was introduced on stage with his staff. It was truly an elegant night.

We had fine dining every night. You can order anything or everything on the menu so I never understood why anyone would not want to eat in the dining room, as opposed to going upstairs at the casual dining, (a buffet which I refer to as the "trough" or the "pitch till you win").

We always loved the variety and you could try a dish you hadn't tried before. If the waiters noticed you were not eating a dish, they would offer to get you something else. Needless to say, the service was excellent.

The ships have wonderful shows featuring very talented singers and dancers. Their production shows have been known to have thirty different scenes and costume changes. Yes, I counted.

I took a few 5 day cruises over the years, but 7 days is the best bargain. If I have to fly to a port, I want to get as much for my money as possible and it wasn't worth it to me to fly to California or Florida for just a 5 day cruise.

These days there are ports in so many cities, but when I started cruising you had to go to Miami or Los Angeles.

I cruise out of Galveston, Texas or New Orleans, Louisiana quite often because we can drive to either port from Little Rock in about eight hours.

They have ports in Tampa, Port Canaveral, Miami, Ft. Lauderdale, New York, Mobile, San Diego, Los Angeles, Seattle, Galveston, New Orleans, Baltimore, Charleston, and San Juan. I've probably missed some of the newer ports and this is only Carnival Cruise Line.

My son Joe was 9 years old on our first cruise and one of only 12 children on the entire ship. Cruising wasn't as affordable or as common in those days. We paid more per person than what you would pay for a suite these days and we had an inside cabin on the old Mardi Gras.

On the older ships the comedians would joke about the small bathrooms. It was said that you could sit on the toilet, take a shower and shave at the same time. We never tried that, but trust me, it was possible. The "shower curtain" encompassed the sink, and toilet.

On the Mardi Gras there was a slot machine room on the same floor as our cabin. My son Joe could go in there and actually play the slots although he wasn't allowed in the big casino.

They also allowed everyone in the Disco. Joe would go to the disco, order a coke and watch the dancing. Nobody cared what he did. One of the things he said he loved most about cruising was the freedom he had to come and go. He felt like an adult.

The waiters are always attentive and give great service, but when you had a child with you, they go out of their way to take care of the wants and needs of your children. They would even cut up their food if they needed help.

For a Mom, this was a true vacation. No cooking, no cleaning, no taking care of your kids... just being pampered and relaxing. I loved it!

I hadn't intended to do a chapter selling cruises, but since I was telling you some of the features of cruising, I might as well give those of you that haven't ever cruised, a little more information.

Cruising is and always has been the best vacation buy ever. The prices are so affordable you can go as a couple, a family or have a family reunion on a cruise. One of the great things about taking a cruise with a group is you can spend as little or as much time together as you want.

Some families take their evening meals together but do their own thing during the day. There is such a variety of activities on the ship as well as meal choices, you can cruise together, but not "be together" every waking moment.

So if Aunt Bertha drives you crazy, you don't have to see her or be with her every minute of the day or night. You might want to lay out in the sun and Aunt Bertha might want to go to a class on how to make towel animals, while Uncle Charlie might want to go to the casino and your Mom might want to shop for souvenirs.

Carnival Cruise Line has what they call "Camp Carnival" for the kids. They are entertained and cared for and are never bored. They make new friends and absolutely love it, while giving their parents a break from being a "Mom" (or Dad).

All meals, entertainment and activities are included in the cruise price, so you get your accommodations, travel, shows, meals and transportation to the various ports at one low price.

Alcoholic drinks, casino, shopping and purchasing pictures (and you will want your ships pictures) are at additional cost.

The easiest way to book a cruise is either on the website of the cruise line or calling the cruise line and booking it over the phone.

They offer discounts at times for military (or retired military) law enforcement, seniors or past guests. Always "ask" if they have a promotion for any of these categories.

You can make a small deposit and you have till forty five days before your cruise to pay it off. When you are onboard you will be issued a "Sail and Sign" card and that will be all you need to have with you. Any purchases go to your account and is guaranteed by either "cash" you put in your account or will be charged to your credit or debit card at the end of the cruise. This card is also your room key.

The new Carnival ship coming out in 2020 is going to be named the Mardi Gras. The original Mardi Gras was retired years ago but they are bringing back the name for their newest ship.

The ship will be 180,000 tons and will carry 5,286 passengers. Talk about a huge difference in cruising in the last 39 years.

When we heard about the new Mardi Gras we were so excited and I've already booked a cruise on it. It will be "40 years" from our first cruise when we go on the new Mardi Gras. This will be a very special and sentimental cruise for us. I can't wait.

MY CRUISE HISTORY

Date	Ship	Port	Length
May 1980	Carnival Mardi Gras	Miami	7 day
Sept. 1981	Carnival Tropicale	L.A.	7 day
May 1985	Norwegian MS Sunward	Miami	5 day
June 1989	Carnival Carnivale	Miami	5 day
Dec. 1990	Carnival Jubilee	L.A.	7 day
May 2002	Carnival Sensation	Tampa	7 day
Nov. 2002	Carnival Inspiration	Tampa	7 day
Nov. 2003	Carnival Conquest	N.O.	7 day
Dec. 2005	Carnival Liberty	Miami	7 day
Aug. 2006	Carnival Holiday	Mobile	5 day
Sept. 2007	Carnival Triumph	N.O.	7 day
Nov. 2008	Carnival Liberty	Miami	7 day
May 2009	Carnival Ecstacy	Galveston	5 day
Jan. 2010	Carnival Splendor	L.A.	7 day
May 2010	Rhapsody of the Seas	Seattle	7 day
Jan. 2012	Carnival Elation	N.O.	5 day
Nov. 2012	Carnival Magic	Galveston	7 day
Jan. 2013	Carnival Conquest	N.O.	7 day
Oct. 2013	Carnival Magic	Galveston	7 day
Jan. 2014	Carnival Sunshine	N.O.	7 day
Aug. 2014	Carnival Dream	N.O.	7 day
Oct. 2014	Carnival Splendor	New York	8 day
Feb. 2015	Carnival Dream	N.O.	7 day
Nov. 2015	Carnival Dream	N.O.	7 day
Jan. 2016*	Carnival Triumph	Galveston	5 day
Jan. 2016*	Carnival Triumph	Galveston	4 day
July 2016	MS Rotterdam	Barcelona	12 day
Sept. 2016	Carnival Breeze	Galveston	7 day
Nov. 2017	Carnival Triumph	N.O.	6 day
March 2017	Adventures of the Seas	San Juan	10 day
Oct. 2018	Carnival Dream	N.O.	7 day

Dec. 2018	Carnival Vista	Galveston	7 day
Jan. 2019	Carnival Splendor	L.A.	14 day
Oct. 2019	Carnival Horizon**	Miami	8 day
Oct. 2020	Carnival Mardi Gras**	Port Canaveral	7 day

* Back to Back Cruise   ** Future cruises already booked

CITIES I'VE VISITED IN 2½ YEARS

(Numbers indicate how many visits to same city)

San Juan, Puerto Rico (2)
Bayamon, Puerto Rico (2)
St. Thomas - U.S. Virgin Islands
Antigua, Independent Commonwealth
St.Lucia, Eastern Caribbean
Barbados, Eastern Caribbean
Bonaire - Dutch Caribbean
Curacao - Dutch Caribbean
Aruba - Dutch Caribbean
Toronto, Canada
Niagara Falls, Canada
Montego Bay, Jamaica (3)
Grand Cayman, Cayman Islands (3)
Roatan, Honduras, Central America
Belize, Central America
Las Vegas, NV (4)
Grand Canyon, Arizona
Puerto Vallarta, MX (4)
Phoenix, AZ
Sacramento, CA
Auburn, CA
Reno, NV (2)
Panama City, FL
Orange Beach, FL
Destin, FL
New Orleans, LA (2)
Cancun, MX (2)
Isla Mujeres, MX (2)
Cozumel, MX (5)

Playa Del Carmen, MX (2)
Cabo San Lucas, MX
Mazatlan, MX
Progresso, MX
Branson, MO
London, England
Paris, France
Dublin, Ireland
Glasgow, Scotland
Freeport, Bahamas
Nassau, Bahamas
Houston, TX
Galveston, TX (2)*
Shreveport, LA
Dallas, TX
Paradise, TX (2)*
New York, NY
Atlantic City, NJ
Reno, NV (2)
Carson City, NV
Virginia City, NV
Orlando, FL
Kissimmee, FL
Tampa, FL
St. Petersburg, FL
Cocoa Beach, FL
Rome, Italy
Barcelona, Spain
Cadiz, Spain
Gibraltar, UK Territory
Malaga, Spain
Alicante, Spain
Palma de Mallorca, Spain
Marseille, France
Calvim Corsica, France
Monte Carlo, Monaco

Florence, Italy
Pisa, Italy
Civitavecchia, Italy
Los Angeles, CA
Long Beach, CA
Maui, HI
Honolulu, HI
Hilo, HI
Ensenada, MX

CRUISES IN RETIREMENT THE LAST 2½ YEARS

My first cruise was a 12 day Mediterranean Cruise on the **Rotterdam** of the Holland America Cruise Line.

My second was with my friend\co-worker Rebecca, on a 7 day cruise on the **Carnival Breeze** out of Galveston to Belize, Honduras and Cozumel.

My third was with my friend\co-worker Tammy, on a 7 day cruise on the **Carnival Dream** out of New Orleans to Jamaica, Grand Cayman and Cozumel.

My fourth was a 12 day cruise, sailing alone on the Royal Caribbean cruise **Adventures of the Seas** out of San Juan to the Southern Caribbean.

My fifth was with my friend\co-worker Tammy, on a 5 day cruise on the **Carnival Triumph** out of New Orleans to Progresso and Cozumel.

My sixth was with my son Matt on a 7 day cruise on the **Carnival Dream** out of New Orleans to Jamaica, Grand Cayman and Cozumel again.

My seventh was with my friend\co-worker Rebecca, on a 7 day cruise out of Galveston on the **Carnival Vista.**

My eighth was with Melissa Mitchell, a friend of a friend, on a 14 day cruise out of Long Beach to Hawaii and back on the **Carnival Splendor.**

Made in the USA
Monee, IL
28 February 2022

92024120R00080